The G-man and
the Diamond King

To Phil Walter, FBI
Special Agent and
fellow G-Man, enjoy
and best wishes.

William E. Plunkett 2016

The G-man and the Diamond King

A True
FBI Crime
Story of
the 1930s

William E. Plunkett

ORANGE *frazer* PRESS
Wilmington, Ohio

Published for the author by:

Orange Frazer Press

P.O. Box 214

Wilmington, OH 45177

Telephone: 937.382.3196 for price and shipping information.

Website: www.orangefrazer.com

Book and cover design: Alyson Rua and Orange Frazer Press

Library of Congress Control Number 2015934235

Acknowledgements

This truly was a journey, and a special thank you to John Baskin, my editor, for his patience with a novice. His enthusiasm and interest in the topic certainly made for a far better product.

To the Klein and McGovern family members who provided information, thank you to Richard Klein, Michael McGovern, Eugene Klein, and Dan Gilkey.

Thank you to the FBI associates who provided assistance, encouragement, and inspiration: Monica Leigh Grover, William R. Hargreaves, Kevin G. Hogan, Cynthia Mosby, David Remley, Douglas Roden, Timothy Tracy, Nell Umbaugh, and Larry Wack.

To two young ladies who were not the demographic I was initially thinking about when I started this project, Angela Shinkle and Michelle Johnson: thank you for your proofreading and suggestions with a rough manuscript. Doria Lynch, thank you so much for your wonderful research presentation on the Barrett case, and to Mike Perkins who assisted with news articles and photographs, thank you.

Thanks to my Kentucky traveling guide, Jerry Spradlin.

Finally to my father, Michael H. Plunkett, former Special Agent, Alcohol, Tobacco & Firearms, U.S. Department of Treasury, for his continued encouragement.

In memory of Sally and Travis

Contents

We were the vaunted G-men once.... we did our little bit.

Where now we could not qualify to be part of it.

For now the FBI is not the group that it used to be....

It is the model of success and true efficiency.

We had to learn the hard way then the things we did not know....

And as we took our chances great, we helped the Bureau grow.

We suffered heartaches and we lost the lives of several men,

But surely every one of us would do that job again.

Because today the FBI is worthy of its name....

And we are proud and happy that we helped create its fame.

—James J. Metcalfe (FBI 1931–1935), from his poem
"We Were the G-Men"

"You can't just go round killing people whenever the mood strikes you.
It's not feasible."

—Elisha Cook Jr., *Born to Kill* (1947)

Introduction

As an investigator, you're always trying to answer who, what, when, where, why, and how of a given incident. It's one of the reasons I became a Special Agent with the FBI, because cases have a lot of unanswered questions, and at times the full answer and/or the truth is never fully realized. My last—perhaps my most interesting—investigation was not assigned to me; it came about in the oddest of ways.

Each of the fifty-six FBI field offices have a wall of honor dedicated to the Special Agents who died in the performance of duty[*] or as the result of an adversarial action.[†] The wall contains a photograph of the agent who died and a small narrative of how his death happened. During my career with the FBI, I served two tours in the Cincinnati FBI Office, one starting in 1986, the second in 1997. On numerous occasions, I stopped and looked at the wall, which was located near where management was, in what we called "mahogany row." I often looked at the photographs and read the narratives, and I'm sure I read the narrative for Special Agent Nelson B. Klein (the eighth name added to the wall), never knowing until years later that the Cincinnati office was his last assignment. Nelson Klein, at the time, though, was merely a name.

In the fall of 2004, Special Agent Timothy Tracy of the Louisville Division, assigned to the resident agency office in Covington, was reading the October 18, 2004, edition of the *Kentucky Post* when he saw an article written by Jim Weis titled "Before FBI Came G-Men." It was about Nelson Klein, who had been assigned to the Cincinnati FBI Office in 1932 and lived with his family on the second floor of a house on Electric Avenue in Southgate, Kentucky. After he had been killed in 1935, he was buried at Evergreen Cemetery in Southgate. Tracy filed the information away.

Then in 2008, Tracy went to Evergreen Cemetery and found Klein's gravesite in disrepair; it appeared that deer had knocked over the family headstone. Disturbed by this, Tracy contacted the Klein family and asked permission to have the headstone reattached to its base, and a bronze FBI badge—eight inches by six—and the inscription "Nelson B. Klein, Special Agent FBI, Killed in the Line of Duty, August 16, 1935," placed on it. When Lewin Monuments of Fort Mitchell, Kentucky, learned of the project—involving the gravesite of an FBI agent killed in the line of duty—the company immediately reduced its price for the repair and gave a discounted price for adding the new inscription. Company officials said they "considered it an honor to be doing the restoration."[1]

💎 Klein's memorial service was attended by over a hundred officers and family members, 73 years after his murder.

That summer, there was a rededication at Agent Klein's gravesite, organized by the Cincinnati chapter of the Society of Former Special Agents of the FBI (SFSAFBI), who provided the funds for the repair. The ceremony was attended by over a hundred FBI, local law enforcement, and family members. Former Special Agent Larry E. Wack, along with SFSAFBI chapters around the country, then sought out locations where other agents who had been killed in the line of duty were buried, and they made similar repairs and dedications.

The Klein service was melancholy, made more so by the empty plots beside Klein's, which were obviously intended for his family, who had moved away after his death. Klein's widow, Catharine, was deceased, too, and two of his three children. *We should know more about him*, I thought. The service reminded me of what could happen to agents at any time, and it made me think of the difficulties of being an agent in Klein's time. Agents were often called upon at a moment's notice to investigate a case; they traveled long distances, stayed in less than ideal conditions, and dined poorly. Even when being assisted by other agents or local law enforcement, they often found themselves out on a limb. Families didn't know where they were, what they were doing, or when—or if—they would return.

Why did they do it? It was not likely just for money, glory, or even for J. Edgar Hoover. They did it because what they were doing had value; it was bigger than themselves. They

The G-man and the Diamond King

were the pioneers of the organization, and they found themselves in the thick of the dangerous 1930s as the Bureau invented itself, men like Purvis, Connelley, and Harris—all of the Cincinnati office—and all of whom missed the work after they left.

And so began my investigation. Nelson Klein became my case, and Tracy and I went out to find additional facts about what had happened on August 16, 1935. We first tried to locate military, FBI, and court records. The United States Attorney's office in Indianapolis said its prosecution file of George Barrett, the man who had killed Klein, was no longer available. Barrett's FBI file had been destroyed in 1997. Finally, after piecing information together from over a hundred news articles, I got the FBI investigative file of Agent Klein's murder from the National Archives.

I visited the cemetery where Agent Klein was buried, the funeral home where his services were held, and went to Klein's former residence in Southgate. In 2011, Tracy and I went to Liberty, Indiana, to review records and to College Corner, Indiana, to see where the gunfight took place. We found one of George Barrett's cousins, still living in College Corner, who seemed somewhat embarrassed about her family's participation in the sensational murder and subsequent trial, but she was kind and helpful, showing us where everything had happened.

In September of 2013, I went to Big Hill, McKee, and Berea, Kentucky, doing more research on George Barrett. In November of 2014, I again traveled with Tracy, this time to Indianapolis, to attend a presentation on the story of U.S. v George Barrett, which was held at the Birch Bayh Federal Building and the United States Court House. The excellent presentation was given by court historian Doria Lynch, in the same courtroom where Barrett had been tried. The courtroom looks today just as it did then, jury box, witness stand, judge's seat, and stained glass windows and small murals depicting the seals of the original thirteen colonies.

In the 1987 film *Extreme Prejudice*, the actor Rip Torn plays a sheriff who said—talking about a drug dealer—"Funny, ain't it, how it comes around. Right way's the hardest, wrong way's the easiest. Rule of nature, like water seeks the path of least resistance. So you get crooked rivers, crooked men." What follows is the story of two men: one on the side of good, Nelson B. Klein, Special Agent, FBI, and the other, George Barrett, a career criminal, on the wrong side—and how their paths crossed.

The retelling of this story is dedicated to those who carried an FBI badge and put themselves in harm's way.

ENDNOTES

*Performance of Duty: The FBI Honors those employees who lost their lives in the performance of their duty, but not necessarily during an adversarial confrontation. This would include situations involving active performance of law enforcement, investigative, intelligence, or public safety activities. A Performance of Duty death is the direct result of a personal injury sustained while acting in direct response to an employee's FBI task or mission.

†Adversarial Action: The FBI honors its employees killed in the line of duty as the result of a direct adversarial force, or at or by the hand of an adversary. For this subset of those who died in the performance of duty, the death of the employee must have occurred while in the Performance of Duty and be the result of adversarial action. Adversarial action is defined as any antagonistic action or conflict where there is reasonable belief that carrying out one's duty poses possible imminent danger of death or serious physical injury to the employee or to another person.

The G-man and the Diamond King

The G-man and the Diamond King

Prologue
The birth of modern crime-fighting

*I*n the opening years of the twentieth century, crime in America had outdistanced the country's law enforcement efforts. The criminal element was, by and large, hampered only by its own lack of creativity, and for several decades the law played catch-up, for it was mostly local, essentially unskilled, and without technique, wide communication, or even weaponry. It was a good time to be a criminal.

In the late 1800s, America was a vast, unconnected place, its workings intensely local. America was run by its towns, townships, and counties; Washington was still a presence that resided far over the hill someplace. There was not much need—just yet, anyway—for a national police force, and when the government needed enforcement it turned to the Pinkerton Agency, which *was* a national police force. It was also big and powerful, with 2,000 active agents and thousands more who served as reserves. (Its size and power were such that the state of Ohio outlawed it, worried it could be hired out as a private militia.)

Then after the disastrous Homestead strike in Pennsylvania in 1892 when seven strikers (and three Pinkertons) died, Congress outlawed any federal use of the agency. The Justice Department then turned to using Secret Service agents, but Congress didn't like that, either (what it assuredly didn't like was the possibility of the Department using Secret Service agents to investigate them, which it already had, with a prominent U.S. Senator prosecuted for fraud).

Congress, however hadn't reckoned on dealing with Theodore Roosevelt, who became president in 1901 after the assassination of William McKinley. Roosevelt was a naturalist, a force of nature himself, "the country's first environmentalist president." He was a reformer angry about many things, particularly land frauds perpetuated by speculators, and he wanted his own investigative service to do something about it, as well as about other crime and corruption over which the government had no remedy. It might be said that this was the defining moment that led to the invention of the Federal Bureau of Investigation.

Here's the short version: in 1908, Roosevelt called his attorney general, Charles Bonaparte, to the White House. Bonaparte was an old friend and advisor, and he, too, had a progressive mindset. Roosevelt told the AG to create an investigative service inside the Department of Justice, reporting to none but the AG himself. But when Bonaparte asked for Congressional approval, he was told no. Bonaparte laid low, waited until Congress adjourned for the summer, then used a Justice Department expense fund to hire eight Secret Service agents fulltime—as his own investigators. In July, he signed a formal order setting up his new division with thirty-four "special agents." Congress learned about it in December when Bonaparte's somewhat imperious act appeared quietly buried in a few lines of the department's annual report.

Bonaparte's defiant act, which led to the formation of what would become "the world's most powerful law enforcement agency"—as it has been called— may have actually been illegal. (Even Mark Twain had a moment of complaint, saying that Roosevelt appeared ready "to kick the Constitution into the backyard whenever it gets in the way.") But it was certainly true to what Roosevelt wanted. Bonaparte assured Congress he was not building a secret police state, and early in 1909 he sent his boss a thirteen-page letter that justified himself and the new office. This new agency didn't even have a name; Bonaparte just referred to it as a "special agent force."

The American Bonaparte

Charles Bonaparte was an American original, a blueblood who was said to be "the only authentic member of royalty who ever entered American politics"—he was the grandnephew of the Emperor Napoleon I of France. The American Bonapartes weren't part of the dynasty, however, didn't pay any attention to titles, and about the only things that came down to Charles was an aristocratic manner and his heightened sense of self-confidence. He was once described as having "the cannon-ball head of a warrior, with room for two sets of brains." In keeping with his bearing, he wasn't much for public relations. Once when Roosevelt ordered border patrolmen to take target practice, Charles said he would have ordered the men to fire at one another, and given the jobs to the survivors. He was credited with trust-busting the tobacco monopoly, and he was a civil reformer, but he also opposed the public school system. "As ridiculous the State should provide free schools," he once said, "as that it should supply free soup houses!" The press loved that, and Charles found himself saddled with the nickname, "Souphouse Charlie."

George Wickersham succeeded Bonaparte in 1909, and he named his organization formally: the Bureau of Investigation (BOI). Fewer than seventy people worked for it (more than 35,000 people work for today's FBI, including some 13,000 Special Agents). In its early days, there were few federal crimes made into law, which limited the BOI's investigative purview. It primarily investigated violations of laws involving national banking, bankruptcy, naturalization, antitrust, peonage, and land fraud. It provided no formal training to new agents, preferring men with previous law enforcement experience or a background in law.

Its jurisdiction expanded in major fashion in 1910 when Congress passed the Mann "White Slavery" Act, which made it a crime to transport women over state lines for immoral purposes. Its stated purpose was to curb interstate prostitution, but in the national moral panic of the time it was applied politically—according to its critics, at least—when Jack Johnson, the first African-American heavyweight boxing champion was convicted of transporting a prostitute from Pittsburgh to Chicago. Critics of the arrest said that the charges had occurred before the passage of the Mann Act and that the woman was his girlfriend (he later married her); he was convicted by an all-white jury and sent to prison.

Past the Mann Act's controversial nature, its importance seemed to be that the agency now had increased powers, and it was a force to be reckoned with. Soon, the agency had more than three hundred agents who were assisted by approximately three hundred support employees. There were offices across the United States, and each field office operation was run by a Special Agent in Charge (SAC) who reported to headquarters in Washington, D.C. Most field offices were in major cities with several located near the Mexican border where they predominantly investigated smuggling, neutrality violations, and conducted intelligence gathering, mostly connected with the Mexican revolution.

During World War I, the BOI's workload increased— it acquired responsibility for investigating espionage, sabotage, and assisted the Department of Labor by investigating eminent enemy aliens. During the war years, agents with general investigative experience and ability in certain languages enlarged the BOI even more. The BOI gained more influence in 1919 with the passage of the Dyer Act, also known as the National Motor Vehicle Act; now it could prosecute criminals who'd previously evaded the Bureau by driving across a state line. More than any other law, the Dyer Act sealed the FBI's reputation as a national investigative crime-fighting organization.

The original defining moment for the Bureau was the affinity of the two like-minded Harvard men, Teddy Roosevelt and his attorney general. Charles Bonaparte. The next such moment occurred in 1924 when a former head of the Justice Department's Alien Enemy Bureau, J. Edgar Hoover, was named head of the BOI, which, by this time, was plagued by scandal and disarray. His background in the Alien Enemy Bureau was good training, for Hoover was a man who knew his enemies.

When he took over, he had 650 people working for him, including 441 special agents in nine field offices in the larger cities. By the time of the Great Depression, Hoover had tripled the field offices, and he had nine big-city divisional headquarters. Cincinnati was one of them. And it was here, in the Cincinnati office, that a well-appointed young agent named Nelson B. Klein would make a name for himself—although it wasn't one he would have chosen.

Mr. G-Man

J. Edgar Hoover was one of America's great political overlords. Making over an institution in his own image, it became one of the most powerful in the nation, and he held onto this power for nearly half a century. Praised, hailed, vilified and damned—depending upon one's point of view—this one-time Sunday school teacher was still responsible for, better or worse, building the FBI into an unassailably modern crime-fighting organization. Said biographer Kenneth Ackerman, "For most of his life, Americans considered him a hero. He made the G-Man brand so popular that, at its height, it was harder to become an FBI agent than to be accepted into an Ivy League college." He has also been credited with inventing the modern surveillance state. Wrote Pulitzer-Prize winning writer Tim Weiner, "Every fingerprint file, every DNA record, every iris recorded through biometrics, every government dossier on

◆ Director Hoover demonstrates the Thompson submachine gun in 1935.

every citizen and alien in this country owes its life to him. We live in his shadow, though he's been gone forty years…"

When Klein came on agency duty in December of 1926, the BOI had no formal training for him. But the systematic Hoover, busy with rebuilding the entire agency, soon would have. In short order, he streamlined the Bureau, stopped patronage, and implemented a merit system. He liked his agents streamlined, too. He wanted them between the ages of 25 and 35, and he demanded they dress alike—white shirts, plain tie (red was forbidden for its Communist associations), and dark suits. Office files were standardized, and even the layouts of field offices. Hoover wanted his agents to look like agents—rigorously upright, no bushy eyebrows, no odd personal attributes. He'd inherited an operation plagued by scandal, and he was going to scrub it clean and make it over in his own image.

Director Hoover ruled by decree. Agents lived in fear of him. Inspection teams appeared without notice, writing up agents that were late to report for duty. He wanted his agents to have a firm, dry, manly handshake, and agents in training who might face Hoover were advised to "pat their hands on their pants legs." He tolerated no laziness, sloppiness, or departure from the rules, which would be met with an iron hand. The smallest infraction could cost an agent his job.

Those who weathered the storm of the application process were almost always of a similar type. They had Southern origins, and many were from Hoover's alma mater, George Washington University, and the fraternity, Kappa Alpha, as well. The Director's number two man, Harold Nathan, had been an administrator with the BOI since 1917 and the only agent of Jewish decent for years. Hugh Clegg, a Mississippian and attorney from Kappa Alpha, was, like most of the new arrivals rotated between offices during the first few months of his career, but he would rise to the position of assistant director.

It was at the field office level that new agents would encounter police departments that were not enamored with the BOI. The police viewed the agents as unarmed, inept dabblers trying to home in on their jurisdiction. Agents were ridiculed as being college boys. Yet despite the appearance that the agents were all loyal, well dressed and well educated with little law enforcement experience, that wasn't the whole story. Hoover had, under the radar, retained non-lawyers, mainly from the Southwest, who were veteran lawmen. They were a rare breed, gunslingers and cowboys who drank alcohol and chewed tobacco. Hoover cast a blind eye at them, ignoring their lack of conformity for the expediency of getting the job done.

The agency was still oddly named, and confusingly so. Old Wickersham had formally named it the Bureau of Investigation back in 1909, but it was sometimes called "the Division of Investigation." Then in June of 1933, President Franklin Roosevelt mandated a Division of Investigation—to be made up of the old BOI and the Treasury Department's Bureau of Prohibition, That fall, the 18th Amendment died, the Bureau of Prohibition no longer had a mission, and by default the BOI had become the DOI. Within the government, however, there were a number of agencies called "Division of Investigation." Hoover, being Hoover, wanted a distinctive name for his division. Congress bowed to the director, and on March 22, 1935—with the president's signature—it became the Federal Bureau of Investigation.

Agent Klein, already a seasoned, six-year veteran, arrived in Cincinnati in the spring of 1932. Not only was he there for the beginning of the new agency, he was present for the beginning of what was surely the agency's defining—and most dangerous—decade. And while he did not know it, he was there to make part of its history.

13225

John Dillinger managed to look dapper,
even on his wanted poster.

Dillinger, Public Enemies, and the G-man

Merriam-Webster defines gangster as "a member of a gang of criminals: racketeer." Under the term, the dictionary could also have listed George W. Barrett as a synonym. Barrett, known to be active with a gang of bootleggers as early as 1913, was a career criminal, associated with various shady individuals and as ruthless as any of the gangsters who regularly made the front pages of the newspapers in the early 1930s. He was already nicknamed "the Diamond King" by family, friends, and associates—and later by the media—because he often carried a pocketful of diamonds. If he had been a serial bank robber, he might have been as famous as any of the headline-robbing gangsters of his time.

There was a lot of competition for those splashy headlines, though, for the years between the middle 1920s and the end of the 1930s was the era of the gangster, brought about largely by the Eighteenth Amendment to the United States Constitution, which prohibited intoxicating liquors. Americans had just come out of WWI, and they wanted to listen to jazz, dance, drive fast automobiles—and drink. Thousands of Americans defied Prohibition, and no law ever caused such contempt from the American people.[1]

Police agencies were overwhelmed with new cases: organized crime increased in power, and corruption extended into the ranks of law enforcement. The amendment was repealed in 1933 by ratification of the Twenty-first Amendment—the only time in United States history that a constitutional amendment was repealed—but the country would never be the same. Odd to think, but a law had made the country lawless.

Three classic gangster movies came out of the period: *Little Caesar* (1931), starring Edward G. Robinson; *The Public Enemy* (1931) with James Cagney, and *Scarface* (1932), directed by Howard Hawks with Paul Muni in the lead. The gangster in each film faced ultimately his own violence, which was supposed to demonstrate a just reward for the unjust. The audiences, however, as Ina Rae Hark wrote in *American Cinema of the 1930s*, identified with those "who, like themselves, had worked hard to achieve something only to have it capriciously ripped away by the Depression." In this grim period of time, it was hard for the ordinary citizen, beset as he was by economic conditions, not to see the gangster as just another working stiff. [2]

American Caesar

Little Caesar was considered the grandfather of American crime films, and it (and the novel it was based on) was written by W.R. Burnett, a one-time government statistician from Springfield, Ohio. Burnett had tried his hand at realistic novels before moving to Chicago, where he got a job as a hotel desk clerk and met a hit man who gave Burnett a sense of how the bad guys talked. "I had the old-fashioned Ohio ideas about right and wrong," Burnett said, "remorse and all that stuff, which to him was utter nonsense. I'd ask him, after he'd kill guys, leave 'em on the street, how did he feel? And he said, 'How do soldiers feel?' To him it was a war." Burnett forgot Balzac and turned to crime, which for him, really *did* pay. He wrote more than thirty novels and some sixty screenplays in a long career that went through 1963 when he wrote the screenplay for *The Great Escape*, a cult classic that starred Steve McQueen as one of Burnett's typical anti-heroes. Said Ian Hamilton of Burnett, "He had a priceless knack: he knew how tough guys talked." [3]

◆ Little Caesar, by way of Springfield, Ohio.

Whether it was life imitating art or vice—emphasis here—versa, the rise of John Dillinger, Baby Face Nelson, Pretty Boy Floyd, Bonnie Parker and Clyde Barrow (aka Bonnie and Clyde), and others, captured the attention of the American public during the

The G-man and the Diamond King

"Public Enemy Era" of the early 1930s. In the eyes of the public, gangsters were modern day Robin Hood figures, robbing from the rich and hitting back at banks, big business, and government. John Dillinger was suavely good-looking, Pretty Boy Floyd and Baby Face Nelson each had a good nickname (even though both of them hated it), and as for Bonnie and Clyde, there was the famous photograph of Bonnie holding a gun on her cocked hip and smoking a cigar. They all died brutally in 1934 but each left an unforgettable picture that in the public imagination was often more compelling than the heedless lives they actually lived.

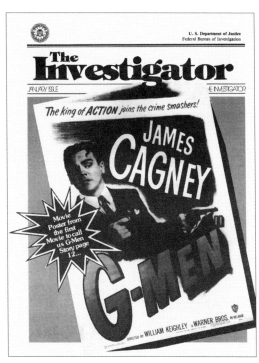

In 1934, Hollywood adopted a self-imposed movie censorship code, the Hays Code, which banned the popular gangster film. The studios got around these new rules by making the crime story about the hero instead of the gangster. In 1935, Hollywood produced sixty-five such films, the most memorable being *G-Men*, starring James Cagney in the title role of FBI Special Agent James "Brick" Davis. The film did not have direct production supervision from the FBI such as there

Cagney as Special Agent makes the cover of the Bureau newsletter.

was in the television series of the 1960s; Director Hoover, according to the Warner Brothers press release, supplied a few technical advisors and approved of Cagney as the leading man. [4]

In FBI mythology, the nickname "G-Men/G-Man" is said to have originated during the arrest of gangster George Celino Barnes, aka "Machine Gun Kelly," in September of 1933 with agents of the Division of Investigation (DOI), the forerunner of the FBI. Realizing that he was unarmed, Kelly supposedly shouted, "Don't shoot, G-Men! Don't shoot, G-Men!" [5] The event was dramatized in subsequent films, such as *The FBI Story* in 1959, which starred Jimmy Stewart, and *Dillinger* in 1973, which featured Warren Oates as the gangster's spitting image. (Dillinger also had a bit part in *The FBI Story*, played by an unknown named Scott Peters, who went uncredited. As the FBI itself would have had it, all the 1930s gangsters—Pretty Boy Floyd, Baby Face Nelson, Machine Gun Kelly, and various hoodlums—had uncredited bit parts. Dillinger himself turned up most recently in the 2011 film, *J. Edgar*, reduced again to a bit part, this time as a death mask kept as a souvenir by Hoover.)

Kelly's wife, Kathryn Throne, exempliflying the old adage that behind every man is a good woman, bought him the Thompson, although Kathryn *wasn't* a good woman. In fact, she may have been worse than Kelly himself. She'd been arrested for, among other things, robbery and prostitution, and with such experience she went to work on Kelly, burnishing his tough-guy image. She was known for handing out spent shell casings, which she called Kelly souvenirs, and she gave him his nickname. Questions remain as to whether Kelly ever killed anyone with a Thompson, or even if he actually said, "Don't shoot, G-Men!" He said it, supposedly, when he was finally apprehended, hung over and still in his pajamas. It sold newspapers, though, and was great public relations.[6]

BANK ROBBERIES: A GROWTH INDUSTRY IN THE 1930s

Hoover instinctively recognized the power of media and helped to instill in the movie-going public a feeling that society was threatened, and that only his undersized but growing force of crime-fighters stood between the safety of the American public and all the mobsters, vicious murders, and other public enemies.[7]

Between 1925 and 1932, the number of bank robberies soared in the United States in what became known as the "crime corridor" between Texas and Minnesota. In 1934, the federal government found itself in open warfare with violent bank robbers like the John Dillinger Gang. The rise of the bank robber was partly caused by the Great Depression, but it was mostly due to technology outpacing the criminal justice system. The Thompson submachine gun—a faster and more powerful weapon—and the V-8 engine allowed gangsters to out-gun and outrun local law enforcement.[8]

After the Kansas City Massacre on June 17, 1933, a number of Midwest DOI supervisors wrote the Bureau in Washington, requesting additional weaponry for their agents. Director Hoover acted quickly, forming a three-person committee that included T. Frank Baughman,* a famous shooter and firearms instructor. The committee recommended a number of weapons, including the Thompson submachine gun. The Bureau either purchased or obtained from the military approximately eight hundred Thompsons. Most were Model 1921s, converted to the slower and more controllable rate of six hundred rounds per minute, like Model 1928s. Many of them had vertical fore-grips and Cutts compensators (which were used to reduce muzzle climb).[10]

The G-man and the Diamond King

Newport's gift to the world

The Thompson submachine gun was the brainchild of General John T. Thompson, an army brat from Newport, Kentucky, who in 1915 had begun looking for an automatic weapon for the American forces in France. He saw his gun as a hand-held machine gun, the answer to the stationary machine gun of the time, "a trench broom to sweep the trenches," as he put it. Unfortunately, his first guns arrived on the New York docks for shipment two days before the war ended in the fall of 1918. Without bulk military orders, the gun was then marketed singly and sold mail order or in local hardware stores and sporting goods stores. Anyone could purchase a Thompson for a mere $225. It acquired its early notoriety in the mid-1920s in Chicago during local mob wars where it became known as "the Chicago typewriter" or "the Chicago piano," along with other such nicknames, and soon it had become a gangster icon inflated by movies and the popular press. [9]

◆ General Thompson of Newport, Kentucky, presents his masterpiece.

The killing of Dillinger by DOI agents did more to enhance the reputation of the organization than apprehending or killing any other Public Enemy Number One designee. The reward for information leading to his arrest was $5,000 and $10,000 for his capture, an unprecedented amount. The DOI needed a major success, and the public needed to gain confidence in the federal government and federal law enforcement: this signified a turning point for the DOI.

Dillinger came out of a middle-class Indianapolis family. His mother died when he was very young and he lived with his widowed father, who neglected him. He was raised by his sister who was thirteen years older and as a result, he was a troubled teen. In 1922, he was arrested for stealing a new car outside of a church in Mooresville, Indiana. In 1923, he joined the United States Navy and became a fireman third class, assigned to the battleship *USS Utah*. He went AWOL while the ship was docked at the port of Boston, received a court martial, and eventually was dishonorably discharged.[11]

Unable to find work, he started hanging out with Ed Singleton, an ex-con, and in September of 1924, he and Singleton got drunk and mugged Frank Morgan, a grocer and Dillinger family friend. They botched the robbery, and both were arrested. Singleton pled not guilty and ended up getting two years while Dillinger, on the advice of his father, pled guilty, was convicted of assault and battery, battery with intent to rob, and conspiracy to commit a felony. He got joint sentences of two-to-fourteen years and ten-to-twenty years in the Indiana State Prison, but he also got an education in the art of robbing a bank, and from experts.[12]

In May of 1933, after serving eight and a half years, Dillinger was paroled. He wasted no time in applying his new education, and a month later, he and others robbed the New Carlisle National Bank in New Carlisle, Ohio, of $10,000. From that June until July of 1934, the Dillinger Gang robbed banks in Ohio, Indiana, Wisconsin, South Dakota, and Iowa. They killed ten men, wounded seven, robbed police arsenals, and staged three jailbreaks. In 1933, while successfully breaking Dillinger out of the Lima County Jail in Lima, Ohio, Pete Pierpont, a Dillinger gang member, shot and killed Sheriff Jess Sarber.[13]

In January of 1934, Dillinger and other gang members were arrested in Tucson, Arizona, after a fire broke out at the Congress Hotel where they were staying. Dillinger was returned to Indiana to stand trial for the murder of Detective Patrick O'Malley, which happened while the gang was robbing the First National Bank of East Chicago, Indiana. He was housed at the county jail in Crown Point, Indiana, where he tricked the guards with what he claimed was a Colt .38—whittled from wood. He forced them to open the door to his cell, locked up the guards and trustees, grabbed two submachine guns, and—insult to injury—fled in Sheriff Lillian Holley's new Ford V-8.[14]

Crossing the state line between Indiana and Illinois, heading for Chicago, Dillinger violated the National Motor Vehicle Theft Act and a federal complaint was sworn out charging him with the theft and interstate transportation of the vehicle, which was subsequently found in Chicago. This gave the DOI the authority to join the manhunt.[15]

Dillinger had eluded capture a number of times, including the DOI-botched raid in April of 1934 at the Little Bohemia Lodge, about fifty miles north of Rhinelander, Wisconsin. Two agents, W. Carter Baum and J.C. Newman, and a constable were looking into a Dillinger-sighting near the lodge and ended up in a confrontation with Baby Face Nelson, who was holding three locals hostage in their car. Nelson shot Agent Newman in the forehead, Agent Baum was killed, and the constable was seriously wounded. Nelson escaped in the agent's vehicle, leaving the hostages behind.[16]

In the spring of 1934, Charles B. Winstead,[†] a gruff Texas marksman who liked to wear a dirty felt hat and the same blue serge suit, was put in Chicago—along with other Western DOI agents—to help catch Dillinger. Hoover liked the experience of the Texans and thought they'd help Chicago SAC Melvin Purvis and his more inexperienced men.[17]

On the evening of July 22, 1934, Dillinger was attending the film, *Manhattan Melodrama*, at the Biograph

◆ For a brief moment, gunmen like Dillinger defined the decade.

Theater in Chicago, in which, ironically, the main character, a gangster named Blackie Gallagher, resembled Dillinger, although in the end he went to the electric chair. The film starred Clark Gable, and some thought Dillinger even looked like Gable.

Made quickly on a cheap budget, the film was expected to return a profit, but it was not expected to capture the imagination of the American movie-going public as it did. To some of the victims of the Great Depression, however, Dillinger was a celebrity. The success of the film surprised MGM and made major stars of Myrna Loy and William Powell. It also bolstered the success of Gable, MGM's most popular leading man, and one reviewer said the movie gave the proponents of capital punishment a boost because no one wanted to see Clark Gable condemned to death.[18]

A scene at Chicago's Biograph Theatre—Dillinger's last show.

Curiosity-seekers fill the alley where Dillinger died at the hands of agents.

Dillinger was with Polly Hamilton and Ana Campanas, aka Anna Sage. Purvis stood by the front door and signaled Dillinger's exit by lighting a cigar, which he did twice, fearing the agents hadn't seen him. Of the many agents and police officers in the area, only six or so actually saw the signal and took action. Dillinger turned his head and looked directly at the agents as he walked by, glanced across the street, then moved ahead of his female companions. He reached into his pocket but didn't extract his gun, a .380 automatic, before running towards a nearby alley.[19]

He never made it. Agents Clarence O. Hurt, Ed Hollis, and Winstead had fallen behind Dillinger, and when Winstead saw Dillinger go for his weapon, he drew his .45 and fired three times; Hurt fired twice and Hollis once. Dillinger was hit at least four times. Winstead is widely believed to have been the agent who fired the fatal shot, shooting Dillinger in the back of the head at close range.[20]

After the death of Dillinger, Hoover assigned Inspector Samuel Cowley of the DOI's Chicago office to apprehend Baby Face Nelson. In late November of 1934, Agents William Ryan and Thomas McDade spotted a vehicle between Fox River Grove and Barrington, Illinois, matching the description of Nelson's stolen car and containing Nelson; his wife, Helen Gillis; and convict John Paul Chase. Ryan and McDade fired on Nelson's vehicle, hitting the radiator and disabling the car. Nelson returned fire, hit their windshield and forced the vehicle off the road. Inspector Cowley and Agent Hollis arrived; neither was wearing a bulletproof vest. They were fired upon by Nelson and Chase. Chase had an automatic rifle, and Nelson had a Monitor 30.06 rifle that jammed, forcing him to grab a Thompson submachine gun.[21]

The G-man and the Diamond King

Cowley returned fire with a submachine gun, hitting Nelson at least six times in the stomach and chest, lacerating his intestines. Nelson, mortally wounded, fired at Cowley, who was hit twice in the chest and stomach, then rolled over into a ditch. Hollis exited the driver's side of the vehicle, firing a sawed-off shotgun at Nelson and hitting him up and down both legs. Hollis, after emptying his shotgun, pulled his pistol and took cover behind a telephone pole. A bullet from Nelson's Thompson hit Hollis in the forehead. Nelson and Chase escaped in the agents' Hudson, and Hollis died on the way to the hospital.[22]

Cowley was taken to the hospital and died in the early hours of November 28. That same morning, Nelson's body was found in a roadside ditch near a cemetery in Niles Center, Illinois; his body had seventeen bullet wounds.

◆ Mickey Rooney stars as Baby Face Nelson in the 1957 movie.

In 1934, the agency had lost Agents Baum, age 29; Hollis, age 31; and Cowley, age 35, all graduates of Washington, D.C., law schools and family men, but the DOI had also brought down several Public Enemy Number Ones. That brought much wanted attention to the DOI, and the message was plain: the government wasn't just talking war on crime. The army fighting this war was the DOI, an elite organization that was one of the most difficult federal agencies in which to gain entry. Hoover wanted agents who were honest, hard working, with common sense and imagination, and each of them had to pass a strict personality test and thorough background investigation

In 1934, the average age of an agent was 35. They had backgrounds in almost every field imaginable. They were former cowboys and Texas Rangers from the Southwest, and former lumbermen, miners, and railroad workers from the Pacific Northwest. More than 80 percent of the agents—there were nearly five hundred of them by this time— had legal training or had been skilled accountants.

Of them, 344 had university degrees (116 had two degrees, 11 had three, and 3 of them had four). Seventy-four agents had been in law enforcement, and thirty-seven had military experience. Nineteen had been farmers, twenty-one were expert horsemen, and eleven of them had been immigration inspectors. There was also one who knew Indian dialects and had solved a murder on an Indian reservation. There were six pilots and at least one parachute-jumper. Forty-one of them had been teachers (both high school and college), twenty-five were expert swimmers, twenty-six accomplished musicians, and fifty of them spoke another language.

There were any number of boxers, baseball and football players, as well as former State troopers, sheriffs, and police chiefs. One of the agents had been a national pistol champion, two were expert trap shooters, another had been a small arms instructor in the Marine Corps, and there was one aerial gunnery expert.[23]

These agents, though from greatly varied backgrounds, were united by the idea of serving their country as crime fighters. The FBI Motto, "Fidelity, Bravery, Integrity," is traced to brief comments made by Inspector W.H. Drane Lester, the editor of the FBI employee magazine, *The Investigator*, in September of 1935: "At last we have a name that lends itself to dignified abbreviation of the Federal Bureau of Investigation, which quite naturally becomes FBI. In the past our nicknames, which the public are so prone to give us, have been many and varied. 'Justice Agents,' 'D. J. Men,' 'Government Men' are but a few of them, with the Bureau itself incorrectly referred to as 'Crime Bureau,' 'Identification Bureau,' and 'Crime Prevention Bureau.' The latest appellation, and perhaps the one which has become most widespread, is 'G-Men,' an abbreviation itself for 'Government Men.' But 'FBI' is the best and one from which we might well choose our motto, for those initials also represent the three things for which the Bureau and its representatives always stand: 'Fidelity, Bravery, Integrity.'"[24]

George Barrett had not yet made it into the pantheon of heavyweights that captured the headlines of the early 1930s in the Midwest. But his own national notoriety was on its way.

ENDNOTES

*Franklin Baughman, discharged after WWI, went to work with the Department of Justice in 1919, and at the age of 22 he was assigned to the General Intelligence Division, working closely with J. Edgar Hoover whom he knew in law school. Baughman remained a close personal friend of Hoover, and Hoover was Baughman's best man at his wedding. After Hoover became Director, he appointed Baughman a supervisor. His responsibilities directing the headquarters staff rated him as the number three position in the Bureau. When Clyde Tolson became assistant Director, Baughman was assigned to Tolson as an assistant, a short-lived arrangement. He was subsequently appointed in the early 1930s as a firearms instructor at the FBI Academy (probably one of the first instructors) and remained there until 1949 when he retired. Baughman died in Florida on September 8, 1971. (*The FBI: A Comprehensive Guide*)

†Winstead was decorated while serving with the US Army in WWI. He joined the BOI in July 1926, and received a letter of commendation from Director Hoover for his involvement in the killing of Dillinger. Winstead served in FBI Offices in El Paso and Albuquerque, and in 1942 he was reprimanded by Director Hoover for insulting a female reporter, having accused her of being a Communist sympathizer. Hoover transferred him to Oklahoma City; and Winstead, in 1943, allegedly told Hoover to go to hell and resigned. He served as an Army Intelligence and Security Officer during WWII. In the Michael Mann-directed *Public Enemies* (2009), based on the book of the same name, Stephen Lang played Winstead and Johnny Depp starred as Dillinger. According to *Box Office Mojo* in 2010, the films budget was $100 million and earned $214 million at the box office, implying that the public's fascination with gangsters was still alive.

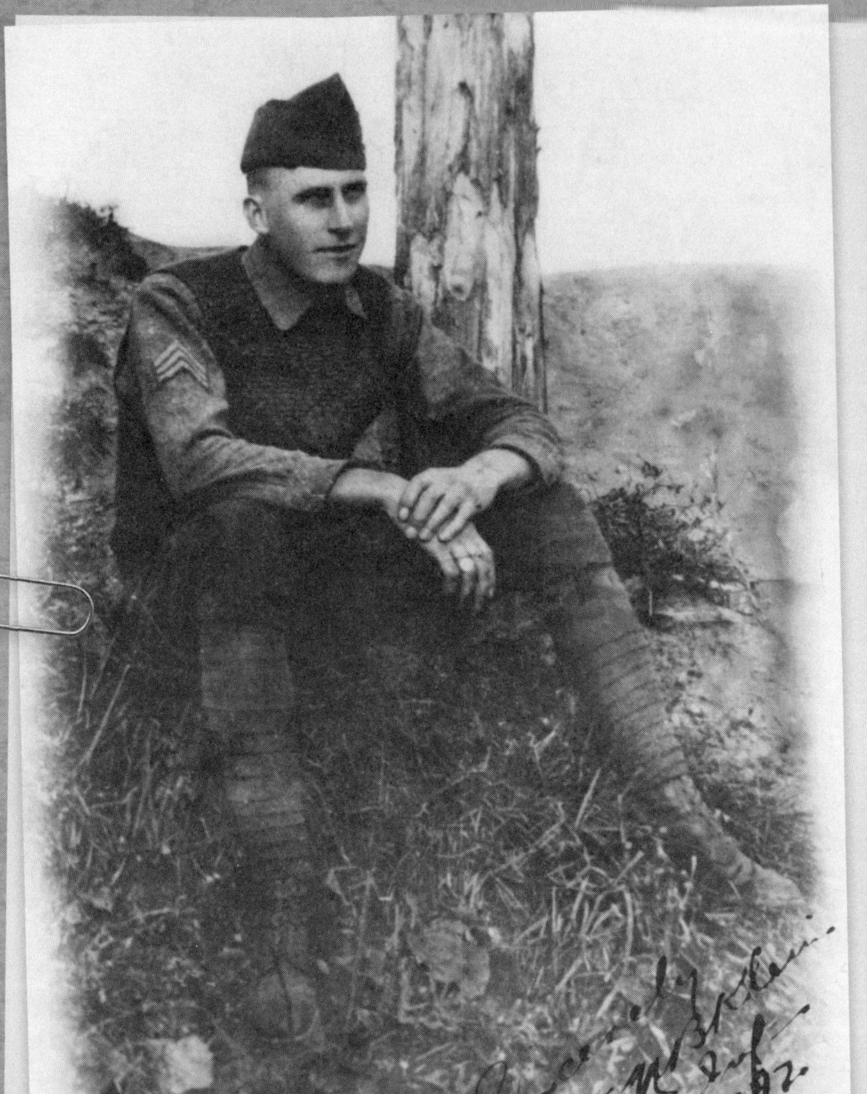

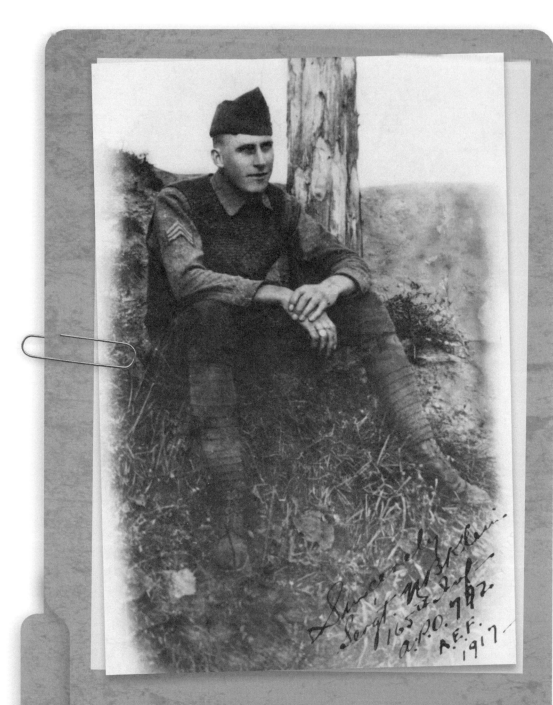

Sergeant Nelson Klein,
in an earlier life.

Nelson Klein, the original agent

Nelson Klein was born on April 3, 1898, in Manhattan, New York. His father, Harry, was employed with Bacon Stevenson & Company, members of the New York Stock Exchange, and his mother, Mary Agnes Creed from Limerick, Ireland, was a homemaker. Klein had an older brother Henry, born 1891, and older sisters Veronica (1893), Bernice (1895), as well as younger siblings Agnes (1899), Eugene (1901), and Victor, born in 1904.

Agnes died in 1912, an event that deeply affected Nelson, who was only a year younger. Eugene, who died in 1998, remembered that he and Victor were playing in their Charles Street house when their father came downstairs with two doctors who were saying that if they had known about Agnes's illness earlier, perhaps they could have saved her. Eugene said Agnes died of scarlet fever and, miraculously, the other children escaped what was, at the time, a major source of childhood mortality.

The Kleins were then living in what was known as the Meat Packing District, a few blocks from the Hudson River, near the West Village and the current New York Police Department's 6th Precinct. For the most part, the Kleins lived on the Lower West Side, but they moved a lot—anytime the rent went up, according to Eugene. They often rented a large house, then rented out spare rooms. They lived for a couple of years in Orange County, New York, on a farm. Nelson would have been 11 or 12 at the time. The children attended a small school there while Mr. Klein worked in New York City. He was listed as a farmer by the 1910 census, but Eugene said his father didn't know a turnip from a tomato. Mrs. Klein, born on a farm in Ireland, had the green thumb in the family, and when they later lived in New Jersey, she always had flowers around the house.

Nelson Klein was raised Catholic but later joined the Episcopalian church. He attended New York public schools, graduated from Grade School Number 95, then attended two years of high school in Boonton, New Jersey. Klein was employed with the Lackawanna Railroad Company in upstate New York as a ticket and station agent, then for a year he took correspondence courses in mechanical drafting, psychology, English, and commercial law from the Coyne School in Chicago until the school closed.

In May of 1918, Klein enlisted in Company A of the 69th New York Infantry and saw service in the New York Guard, where he obtained the rank of sergeant. The New York Guard was born during WWI when the New York National Guard sent a division's worth of soldiers, first for service on the Mexican border, then to fight in France. The New York Guard replaced the National Guard and served as a home guard, mounting guard on the New York City reservoirs.[1] Klein obtained his regimental discharge in April of 1919.

That year, Klein went to work for the Schindler Detective Agency in New York City. The next year, he married Catharine Cox from Mt. Vernon, Ohio, whom he met while she was attending Atlantic City Business College. She was also a bookkeeper at the Ritz-Carlton Hotel in Atlantic City where Klein had worked as house detective. (House detectives at the larger hotels today are known as investigators or house security.) When Klein applied for a position as a Special Agent* with the BOI in 1926, he had served as a house detective for over five years.

Congressman Isaac Bacharach, Second District of New Jersey, wrote a letter to Director Hoover, dated September 29, 1926, recommending Klein for a Special Agent position. Immediately, Hoover sent Klein a letter acknowledging receipt of his application, indicating the application would be placed on file for future reference as there was no current vacancy. On the same day, however, Hoover initiated a background investigation of Klein to determine his suitability for the position.

In early October, SAC John H. Daly interviewed Klein at the BOI field office in Philadelphia, Pennsylvania. The paperwork noted that Klein was 5-foot-11, had a fair complexion, brown hair, and blue-gray eyes. Daly noted that Klein made a good appearance, was neatly groomed, well dressed, and appeared to have an amiable personality. His opinion was that Klein could express himself well and seemed to have wide experience in the meeting of people, although he could not see that Klein had any special qualifications for the Special Agent position. In the past, though, the BOI had hired investigators from various law enforcement agencies, as well as attorneys and accountants.[4]

The G-man and the Diamond King

The greatest detective

Nelson Klein couldn't have found a better man as a model for investigative work. In an era that produced the notable fictional characters of detective work, Raymond Schindler was a real-life one whose work was larger than life. He was born in Mexico, NY, and began his career by selling insurance, then—arriving in San Francisco the day after the famous 1906 earthquake—he answered an ad to do historical research and found, inadvertently he was investigating how much damage had been done to buildings before they were destroyed by fire. He was, therefore, not a historian, as he'd mistakenly assumed; he was an investigator. And how. He became chief lieutenant to William J Burns, the Secret Service man, and when Burns started his soon-to-be famous national detective agency, Schindler ran the New York office as manager. He became noted for his pioneering work with the dictograph and once installed one in a bank spittoon to catch a man blackmailing the bank president. Schindler became famous both for his work, as well as for his night life; he was one of Manhattan's best-known bon vivants, having a reserved table at both the Stork Club and the 21. Rupert Hughes's book, *The Complete Detective*, called him "the greatest detective of the twentieth century," and said "mere fictional detective stories pale in comparison to the real life drama inherent in every one of Ray Schindler's cases."[2][3]

◆ Klein's identification card with Ray Schindler's Detective Agency.

Hoover, meanwhile, received numerous letters of recommendation. Both Inspector James P. Malseed of the Department of Police in Atlantic City and John D. Coughlin of the Detective Division of the New York City Police Department gave Klein high marks, who were believed to be Klein's across-the-aisle law enforcement colleagues. After completing the background investigation and physical exam, Klein was sent a Special Agent appointment letter dated November 24, 1926. The letter indicated a salary of

$2,700 a year with $4 per diem. Klein was administered the oath of office on November 29 by the Chief Clerk of the United States District Court, George Brodbeck, and temporarily assigned to the Philadelphia office.

The temporary assignment was just that, and at 8:55 p.m. on December 10, 1926, he left Philadelphia via the Pennsylvania Railroad, arriving in Portland, Oregon, on Monday, December 13, and reported for duty. The Portland Division was one of the agency's oldest. It had become one of nine divisional headquarters in 1920, and it worked across a range of criminal investigations, from anti-trust issues to prostitution and subversion.

One of its most famous cases occurred in 1935 when George Weyerhaeuser, the nine-year-old heir to the Weyerhaeuser lumber fortune, vanished on his way home from school. Kidnapping had just come under federal jurisdiction with the passage of what was popularly known as the Lindbergh Law in 1932. Young George quickly surfaced, his signature on a ransom note demanding $200,000 in small, unmarked bills. Mr. Weyerhaeuser paid the money, and Portland agents, who had compiled serial numbers, went to work looking for the money to turn up. Within days, the agents had arrested a husband-wife team and identified their ex-con accomplice. All three went to prison in what was called one of the most sensational crimes in Washington state history.[5]

The new federal laws giving agents jurisdiction over the interstate transportation of stolen autos, along with all the division's other duties, made Portland one of the BOI's busiest, and it needed additional agents with investigative experience. When Klein received his first performance review* in January of 1927, the Portland SAC, George Starr, told Hoover that while he'd had only a limited amount of time to observe Klein, he thought Klein was a good agent, that he possessed considerable experience in the field, and displayed high intelligence.[6] It seemed that Klein might be in Portland for some time to come.

On March 31, 1927, Starr graded Klein with an 82 percent efficiency rating, "very good agent work; highly satisfactory."† In April, Klein got a $100 increase in salary—to $2,800 annually.[7] Klein was settling in to his new work in Portland, but the agency had other ideas for him: in May, the BOI sent him back east—to Nashville, Tennessee. There, he received the same kind of marks he'd been getting: Nashville's SAC, J.M. Towler, sent a thirty-day performance letter to Hoover describing Klein as reserved and dignified, with a splendid manner. Towler said that U.S. attorneys in both the middle and eastern districts of Tennessee had met Klein and been favorably impressed. Klein had made several difficult investigative road trips through the eastern mountain districts of both

The G-man and the Diamond King

LCS:EPB

November 24, 1926.

Mr. Nelson B. Klein,
106 Roosevelt Place,
Atlantic City, N.J.

Dear Sir:-

You are hereby notified that you have been appointed a
Special Agent in the Bureau of Investigation, Department of Justice,
with salary at the rate of $2700 per annum, CAF-8. You will also be
allowed your actual expenses of travel and operation and $4.00 per
diem in lieu of subsistence when absent from official headquarters
which are fixed temporarily at Philadelphia, Pa., and following your
general assignment such headquarters will be fixed from time to time
at such places as may be deemed advisable.

This appointment is tendered to you for a probationary
period of three months with the understanding that if your services
are satisfactory at the end of that period the appointment will be
made permanent. It is also understood that you are to proceed on
orders to any part of the country that the exigencies of the service
may require. You should notify this office if this appointment is
accepted by you

Should you accept, you will report to Special Agent in
Charge, J. H. Daly, Federal Building, Philadelphia, Pa., for oath of
office and transportation to Portland, Oregon, where you will report
to Special Agent in Charge, M. Eberstein, Old Post Office Building,
for assignment.

You should so arrange your personal matters, before
taking oath, that you will be able to proceed to any part of the
country for assignment.

Consider this letter strictly confidential. No publicity.

Very truly yours,

67-6822-32

NOV 26 1926

FILE

Enrol.84005

Director.

New agent Nelson Klein receives his first orders from the Bureau.

Nelson Klein, the original agent

Mrs. Firebrand

Mabel Walker Willebrandt was one of the more remarkable figures of the early part of the twentieth century. She was thought to be the first public defender of women, representing prostitutes without pay, and she was legendary among her clients. Once a madam she defended asked about changing her life so that she might raise her sons respectably. After looking into the madam's finances, Willebrandt advised her to work her profession for another six months, then she helped the woman out of her own pocket. She became the U.S. Assistant Attorney General during Prohibition, charged with enforcing the Volstead Act—even when she didn't believe in it. Her private sentiment, however, didn't affect her work: she became even better known for prosecuting the noted Cincinnati bootlegger George Remus. She liked going after the noted bootleggers because, she said, going after the speakeasies "was like trying to dry up the Atlantic Ocean with a blotter." The press called her "Deborah of the Drys," and her friend, John Sirica, who would preside over the Watergate case, said, "If Mabel had worn trousers, she could have been president." At least one biographer said Willebrandt was the one who was most responsible for Hoover becoming director. When Harlan Fiske Stone, the AG, asked her what she thought of him, she said Hoover was "honest and informed and one who operated like an electric wire with almost a trigger response." That reportedly gave Hoover the edge he needed. When Willebrandt died in 1963, the *New York Times* called her "the country's best known woman lawyer," and in 2010, HBO's television series, *Boardwalk Empire*, resurrected her as U.S. attorney Esther Randolph—the role based on Mabel Walker's life.[12][13]

A happy crowd celebrates the return of 3.2 beer in 1933.

Kentucky and Tennessee, and he had made them efficiently and without complaint.[8] In September of 1927, Towler graded Klein with a 91 percent efficiency rating and said that Klein—filling in as Acting SAC in Towler's absence—had developed considerable executive ability.[9]

In March of 1928, Klein picked up another percentage point—Towler graded him at 92 percent. Towler noted that Klein had no legal training but was a good investigator and showed considerable executive ability. The SAC was greatly pleased and recommended Klein for an increase in pay.

In June, Inspector James S. Egan[‡] wrote a memorandum to Hoover concerning his—Egan's—inspection of the Memphis office (headquarters had recently been changed from Nashville to Memphis). Egan said the office was still being operated inefficiently but was in better shape than the last inspection, partly due to the Acting SAC, Klein.

Klein's next transfer was to the Charlotte office, and in August of 1928 the Charlotte SAC reported to Hoover that Klein had been assigned to three bankruptcy matters and that he had performed well on all of them.

Early in 1929, Director Hoover wrote Klein, thanking him for taking only twelve days of leave in the previous year. "I want to express to you my appreciation of the devotion to duty in regard for the interest of the Bureau which impelled this manifestation of loyalty on your part," Hoover said.[10]

In May of 1929, Director Hoover sent a letter to the SAC of the Charlotte office saying the Bureau had received a communication from Assistant Attorney General Mabel Walker Willebrandt regarding the investigation of Joseph Bromberg of Charleston, South Carolina, by Agent Klein. Mrs. Willebrandt requested that the Director express her appreciation to the Charlotte field office for the thorough, to-the-point reports submitted. Hoover said he was pleased to receive commendations of this kind about the work of his agents, and that a notation was being placed in Klein's personnel file.[11]

THE STRANGLING OF VIRGINIA McPHERSON

In September of 1929, the body of Virginia McPherson, a 21-year-old nurse originally from South Carolina, was found by her husband, a bookkeeper named Robert McPherson Jr., in her Park Lane apartment. Her death occurred only a few days after the couple had agreed to separate. They had been married only sixteen months.

Nelson Klein, the original agent

The bedroom door was blocked by her body, clad only in a gauzy negligee and the top of her silk pajamas. The cord of her silk pajama top, according to one report, had been twisted around her neck five times and tied in a surgical knot.[14] [15]

The police were called and after examination by the coroner—and interviewing only one witness—Virginia McPherson's death was ruled a suicide. Policeman Robert J. Allen, an audacious, Cornell-educated lawman, thought the facts showed otherwise, and the decision of suicide a rush to judgment. Allen verbally charged the Third Precinct and the detective bureau with mishandling the evidence and suggested he had information that she was murdered.[16]

"McPherson case shakes up Capital," screamed one headline. It was considered one of the most sensational cases in Washington's history, a mystery, wrote the *Washington Post*, "which has thrown the entire Capital into a seething turmoil, disrupted the Police Department, brought many a sleepless night to the most skilled operatives of the Department of Justice, and to newspaper reporters who have written hundreds of thousands of words about the case."

The grand jury indicted McPherson on a charge of first-degree murder. Testimony was given that the couple had a disagreement on Tuesday and had agreed to separate prior to McPherson's last visit with his wife, which was on Thursday. McPherson's mother said that she received a telephone call from her daughter on Thursday, during which McPherson said she wanted her husband back but a reconciliation couldn't be worked out. "I'm going away and you won't see me anymore," she told her mother.[17]

The grand jury also condemned the police investigation, which resulted in the removal of Inspector William S. Shelby, chief of the detective bureau, and Lieutenant Ed Kelly, the head of the homicide squad. This caused the United States Attorney to ask for BOI assistance with the investigation. Inspector Thomas F. Cullen and fourteen BOI agents were assigned to the matter, and for seven weeks they worked around the clock, interviewing more than eight hundred witnesses and taking almost four million words of testimony.[18]

Allen, the impetuous policeman who'd challenged his bosses' handling of the case, was suspended, however—even though it appeared that the investigation might have died without his insubordination. The *Free Lance-Star* in Fredericksburg said it wasn't the first time "in his stormy career as a police private he was suspended after publishing accusations that his superiors had attempted to whitewash the mystery for the sake of their records."[19]

Klein was part of the BOI interviews, perhaps because of geography: agents from his Charlotte office exhumed McPherson's body, which had been sent back to her home state

The G-man and the Diamond King

for burial. (The place of interment in Chester, South Carolina, was just across the state line from Charlotte.) Klein ended up in Washington, following undeveloped leads and talking to McPherson's neighbors about the night of the murder, as well as interviewing Mr. McPherson's friends. (McPherson was an amateur football player, and his teammates furnished his alibi.)

On October 22, the Department of Justice released the report of the second autopsy, which had been performed at Kannapolis, North Carolina, by Dr. James I. Bullitt, professor of pathology at the University of North Carolina. The autopsy report said there was "no skull fracture, broken neck, illegal operation, or other possible cause of death—only the effect of the pajama cord wrapped tightly around McPherson's throat." [20]

The second grand jury in the McPherson case, in November, heard 106 witnesses and exonerated McPherson in his wife's death by a vote of nineteen to four. The newspaper headlines had been sensational, with rumors and allegations swirling around the case including: infidelity on the part of Mrs. McPherson with a previous friend, Dr. Thomas Ballard; an official police report of a suicide attempt; information from a female nurse friend that she was a lesbian; $1,000 missing from her bank account; her husband being physically abusive and stealing her money to buy alcohol—and, finally, information that she was being blackmailed to provide illicit drugs to an unknown male. McPherson was released after having been in the Washington, D.C., jail since October 4. No one else was ever indicted, and it is unknown whether officials went back and ruled her death a suicide. [21]

In early 1932, Klein was transferred yet again, this time from Charlotte to the agency's Birmingham office. By then, he had gained valuable experience in a broad range of investigative classifications: theft from interstate shipment, veteran bureau matters, impersonation, bankruptcy, intimidation of witnesses, and perjury.

Klein went alone to Birmingham in February. His wife was expecting in April, and Klein thought it unwise that she make the trip with him, going instead to stay with her parents in Mt. Vernon, Ohio. He wrote Hoover, explaining the situation, and asked if he might be transferred to the Cincinnati office, which was relatively near Mt. Vernon. Klein said he had no desire to burden the Director with his family problems, and he was not dissatisfied with his transfer to Birmingham, but he wished to be near his wife during the pregnancy and would be greatly appreciative if the Director might be able to arrange a transfer.

Hoover responded to Klein's transfer request on March 25, indicating that his request was being recorded on the bureau's preference list.§ The Director went on to say that "when conditions permit, the request would be given his further personal consideration." [22]

At the end of March, the Birmingham SAC gave Klein an efficiency rating of 90 percent. The SAC said Klein seemed to have a sensitive understanding of the bureau's work. He was thorough and accurate, qualified to perform all types of investigations, including antitrust and bankruptcy investigations. He had learned to type, and he was enrolled in the bureau's accounting course. [23]

Hoover obviously thought that the needs of the BOI and the Klein family coincided, for Klein was transferred to the Cincinnati office and reported for duty on April 6, 1932. In May, the Cincinnati Office Acting SAC, W.A. Rorer,[||] provided Hoover with Klein's thirty-day report. It found Klein's work highly satisfactory. He required a minimum amount of supervision, had an excellent knowledge of the investigative and administrative manuals, and was energetic and efficient. Klein was considered to be an above-average agent. [24]

Hoover received a memorandum, also in May, from Inspector Vincent Hughes, a technical man who'd been in the BOI even before Hoover, telling the Director that the U.S. attorney for South Carolina's western district had called him, saying how impressed he'd been with the quality of the young agents with whom he'd come in contact during the past two years, and he was particularly complimentary of Agent Klein. [25]

Then in October of 1933, Inspector Hugh H. Clegg[#] submitted a memorandum to the Director marked personal and confidential concerning Agent Klein. The letter acknowledged that Klein was the number one man at the Cincinnati office, and that he reported for temporary duty from October 9 to October 14 in 1933, assuming the duties of acting SAC at the Washington, D.C., office. Clegg called his report, "sad in its nature and sorrowful in its indications." Clegg wrote of Klein serving as acting SAC in Memphis, Charlotte, and Cincinnati, and said by Klein's own admissions, he'd never had any SAC point out his deficiencies or offer any constructive advice. [26]

Clegg said it was particularly unfortunate in view of the fact that Klein, when entering duty, was not qualified as an attorney or an accountant, and he needed guidance and sympathetic instruction to overcome such a handicap. On October 17, 1933, Hoover wrote, at the bottom of Clegg's letter, "This is a sorry commentary on our SACs. I think a letter should be prepared at once to all SACs, calling attention to this condition as observed by Clegg, which is apparently universal in our service." [27]

On March 31, 1934, the SAC of the Cincinnati office, E. J. Connelley, graded Klein at an efficiency rating of 87 percent. He said Klein was a capable agent, could handle all classes of cases, and was receiving additional training in antitrust work. Klein had testified in United States District Court and before the grand jury but had not been observed by

The G-man and the Diamond King

SAC Connelley. Klein, he said, had a reasonable degree of executive ability and filled in as the number one man in SAC Connelley's absence from the Cincinnati office. [28]

In May, Connelley wrote Hoover about Klein's qualifications in the handling of firearms. Klein had qualified as a marksman—or better—with a pistol and had been instructed in the use of the revolver, machine gun, shotgun, high-powered rifle, and tear gas equipment. Connelley said Klein had been on one raid with him and he was qualified to use the equipment in question under trying conditions. [29]

THE LABATT INVESTIGATION

On August 14, 1934, John Sackville Labatt, president of the Labatt Brewing Company, was returning to his office in London, Ontario, from his cottage on Lake Rosseau near Bracebridge. Soon after leaving, his car was forced to a stop by another vehicle, and Labatt was abducted at gunpoint. He was forced to write a letter to his brother Hugh, telling him to go to the Royal York Hotel in Toronto to await further instructions. Labatt was then taken to a cottage on Lake Muskoka where he was blindfolded and chained to a bed. [30]

The kidnappers were Michael Francis McCardell—known as "Three-fingered Abe"— John "Jack" Basil Bannon, Albert Pegram, and Russell Knowles. Hugh went to the Royal York and began gathering money to pay the ransom; word got out and the media gathered at the Royal York. By August 15, the Labatt kidnapping was front-page news across both Canada and the United States. The $150,000 ransom demand was triple the amount Charles Lindbergh had paid in 1932 for the return of his kidnapped baby son, who was subsequently found murdered. The Labatt kidnapping was the first in Canadian history of someone well known.[31w]

The kidnapping of brewery executive John Labatt provides 1934 headlines.

Nelson Klein, the original agent

The publicity caused the kidnappers to panic, so he was unchained from the bed after three days of captivity and driven to Toronto, where he was released on St. Clair Avenue in the Forest Hill neighborhood. The kidnappers gave him cab fare, then fled. Labatt went to the Royal York hotel to meet his brother, Hugh. It took a few moments for the crowd of reporters to realize who had just walked in the door, then pandemonium erupted.

Arthur Roebuck, the attorney general of Ontario, contacted Director Hoover to have the BOI assist in the investigation. Klein, along with Howard D. Harris from Cincinnati, assisted Canadian officials when they sought David Meisner and Kingdon "Piccolo Pete" Murray in Covington, Kentucky, in connection with the case.[32] That, however, was a case of mistaken identity: Meisner faintly resembled Knowles and was falsely picked out of a lineup by Labatt, convicted, and sentenced to fifteen years. He served a year, obtained a second trial, and was acquitted. Murray served seven months and was released, based on testimony from the real kidnappers.[33]

Bannon and McCardell were arrested and charged with kidnapping and armed robbery. Knowles was charged with kidnapping, armed robbery, and extortion—he had later sent extortion letters to the Labatt family. McCardell received a twelve-year sentence, Bannon and Knowles received fifteen. They all served their time at Kingston Penitentiary in Kingston, Ontario, now a national historic site. Bannon and Knowles obtained early release in 1943. Pegram was never found. Labatt continued his business and civic activities after his ordeal. His family was concerned for him as he had a weak heart, and they thought the strain would cause him to have a heart attack, which eventually happened in 1952 when he was 72.

On March 29, 1935, I.A. Humphries, deputy attorney general of Ontario, sent Hoover a thank-you note: "On behalf of the attorney general and his department, I wish to extend to you our appreciation for the courtesy and assistance that was rendered to officials of this department by two of your agents, namely, H.D. Harris and N.B. Klein of Cincinnati. I might also mention Mr. Larsen, who is the agent in charge of the Criminal Investigation Branch at Detroit. It is indeed most gratifying to have such excellent co-operation from these gentlemen."[34]

THE KIDNAPPING OF ALICE STOLL

In the fall of 1934, Agent Klein assisted in the investigation of the Alice Speed Stoll kidnapping, which took place outside of Louisville, Kentucky, on the afternoon of October 10, 1934. She was the wife of Berry V. Stoll, vice president of the Stoll

Oil Refining Company and niece of Fredrick M. Sackett, a United States senator from Kentucky and former ambassador to Germany.

The kidnapper posed as a telephone repairman to gain access to the residence, beat Stoll, forced her into a car, leaving a typed, two-page, legal-size ransom note demanding $50,000. The ransom note requested that the money be placed in a small box and shipped by Railway Express to a neutral party within five days. The name Thomas H. Robinson of 1716 Ashwood Avenue, Nashville, Tennessee, was hand printed at the bottom of the page; other printing in the margin indicated that Berry Stoll was the original target.[35]

On October 20, Chicago SAC Melvin Purvis of Dillinger case fame

Kentucky heiress Alice Stoll's kidnapping provides Klein with an early headline case.

(Klein also participated in this investigation) arrived in Cincinnati with some of his men, lying low at the Alms Hotel to keep the media from getting wind of why they were in town. Purvis—who had previously been appointed SAC in the Cincinnati office in 1931—knew the Ohio territory and with the combined manpower of Chicago and Cincinnati agents, he felt confident in Robinson's apprehension. Purvis, however, received a telephone call from Cincinnati Acting SAC Howard Harris, that Pretty Boy Floyd was believed to be in the vicinity of Wellsville, Ohio. Purvis and his men left Cincinnati to pursue Floyd, who was "Public Enemy Number One" at the time. Meanwhile, around this time, Klein and his fellow agents had been pursuing Robinson, allegedly spotted in Springfield, Ohio. Klein's pursuit of Robinson took him all over the East Coast and Midwest, just missing the elusive kidnapper a number of times.[36]

The kidnapper proving elusive, particularly so because he frequently masqueraded as a woman. (Said the usually austere *New York Times*, "his penchant for dainty girlish garb led to his eventual downfall," and *Time* magazine's headline was "Absent Transvestite.")[37]

Nelson Klein, the original agent

The G-Man's G-Man

By simply doing his job, it seemed that Melvin Purvis became the face of the Bureau in the 1930s. He presided over the manhunts that brought to bay those legendary gangsters, Dillinger, Nelson, and Floyd. He was "the Man Who Got Dillinger," even though he never fired a shot (indeed, some accounts said that he never fired a shot in his career as an agent). But the media liked his unassuming manner, and he received fan mail from all over America

(including proposals of marriage). He became the Bureau's poster boy and a household name, but in Director Hoover's shop, that was no place to be. When he left the Bureau, he was seen as a national hero, the very personification of the quelling of 1930s violence. Most accounts placed his leaving on Hoover, who wanted the agency to remain faceless; if it *were* to have a face, it would be Hoover's. The Director even undermined Purvis's attempts to work, and Purvis turned to what he considered humiliating commercial endorsements.

◆ In 1931, Melvin Purvis became SAC of the first Cincinnati office; a year later he was put in charge of the Chicago office.

He died in 1960 from a gunshot wound to the head. It was called a suicide but later reports said it was an accident, that Purvis was trying to dislodge a tracer round. Hoover didn't attend the funeral or send condolences, but the widow wrote Hoover. "We are honored that you ignored Melvin's death," she said. "Your jealousy hurt him very much but until the end I think he loved you." [38] [39] [40]

On May 11, 1936, Robinson was arrested by BOI agents in Glendale, California; he had in his possession a .38 caliber revolver. Agents had been put on Robinson's trail by a Pasadena druggist who'd found Robinson's masquerade suspicious. Said the druggist, "Her voice was pretty low for a girl." The *New York Times* called Robinson the last of the "Public Enemies Number One," after he'd risen to that spot by attrition: the G-men had earlier nabbed Alvin "Creepy" Karpis (who'd threatened to kill Hoover); and William Mahan, the Weyerhaeuser kidnapper. Robinson was quoted as saying about his captors, "Well, I expected it from these fellows." [41]

Both father and son, along with Robinson Jr.'s wife, were indicted for the kidnapping. Robinson Sr. was tried and acquitted. Robinson Jr. was sentenced to life in prison, serving his first nine years in Alcatraz. He was released from prison in 1970 whereby he obtained Social Security card 255-96-5441 in the state of Georgia, and he died in 1994 at age 87 at Pegram, Tennessee.

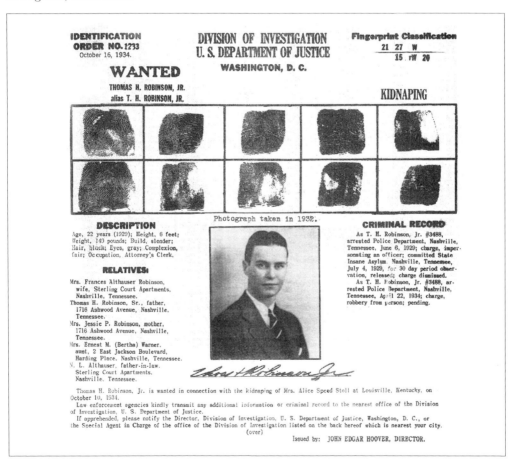

♦ The slender clerk Robinson, shown here in the agency's wanted poster, looks anything other than menacing.

Nelson Klein, the original agent

It seemed as if Klein was finally getting some of the training that Inspector Clegg had complained to Hoover about. The Director himself sent a memo to Assistant Director Tolson in March that read: "This afternoon I saw Mr. N. B. Klein, assigned to the Cincinnati office of the bureau, who is at present attending the retraining school. Mr. Klein seemed to be a particularly serious-minded agent…His whole attitude is that of a person who is particularly interested in his work and in making good in the tasks which he has to perform. I believe that he also has some executive ability." [42]

In April, Inspector Clegg sent a memo to Hoover about Klein attending the four-week retraining class. He wasn't as effusive as the Director. Although Klein had earned a 93 percent on the written examination, Clegg, still hedging his bets, said that Klein was a practical type of agent and seemed to possess determination. He told Hoover he thought Klein's ability as an investigator was "somewhat above average." [43]

In May of 1935, the Cincinnati SAC, E. J. Connelley, gave Klein an efficiency rating of 88.5 percent. He pronounced Klein a capable employee with considerably better-than-average ability. He could handle all classes of cases, created confidence in others, and was personable. He was willing, industrious, and qualified in the handling of firearms. Connelley said that he believed Klein could give a very satisfactory account of himself in any dangerous assignment, particularly where firearms were used, due to his coolness and maturity. [44]

◆ The Bureau had its Cincinnati offices here in 1935, in the U.S. Customs House and Post Office Building.

The G-man and the Diamond King

DONALD CONRAD MCGOVERN

In 1935, the Cincinnati FBI Office was located at the U.S. Customs and Post Office Building, on 5th Street between Main Street and Walnut, and a squad of approximately twelve agents was assigned to the office. Klein's partner that year was Agent Donald C. McGovern, a Pennsylvania native who at age nine lost his father in a lumber mill accident. His mother then moved the family to Jacksonville, Florida, where she ran a boarding house and later a golf course. McGovern had dropped out of high school to help support the family.

He didn't give up on his education, however. He returned to school and eventually graduated from the University of Florida with both a bachelor's degree and a degree in law. He worked as a salesman, radio announcer, a hotel and railroad clerk, and also had two years of legal experience. McGovern applied for the Special Agent position with the DOI because it was the only quality employment he could find at the time.

In March of 1934, he was interviewed for a DOI position by Inspector T.D. Quinn at Charlotte, North Carolina. Quinn was impressed with McGovern, believed that he would make a good agent, and recommended him. McGovern entered on duty in

◆ Donald McGovern, Klein's young partner in the Cincinnati office.

April at Washington, D.C., at a salary of $2,900 a year. In May, he and sixteen other trainees qualified in the use of the .38 Special Police Positive revolvers, with McGovern qualifying as a sharp shooter, and he and the other trainees received additional firearms training in the use of the gas gun, Thompson Sub-Machine Gun, shotgun, and Colt Monitor Machine Gun. His instructor rated his overall prospect at becoming a successful Special Agent as "fair," describing him as being very talkative with a youthful ego, which the instructor felt he had overcome.[45]

He reported for duty at the Cincinnati office on May 24. His first fitness for duty report to Hoover described him as being slight in build (5-foot-8, 135 pounds), of average intelligence, and was somewhat immature. He was enthusiastic about his work but slow to comprehend. He covered investigative assignments logically, appeared to respond well to suggestions and criticism, and it was believed he would develop into an average agent but quite possibly not an outstanding one.[46]

His sister, Margaret Gilkey, was recently widowed and moved with her two sons to Cincinnati to live with her brother on Madison Road in Cincinnati. McGovern was fond of her son, Robert. Robert married Ruth E. Gilkey, who currently resides with her son Dan in Cincinnati.

On June 22, 1935, a memorandum from Assistant Director Clyde Tolson to Hoover recommended that McGovern be suspended without pay for three days and censured for the loss of his bureau-issued Colt revolver. A week or so earlier, before leaving for Dayton, McGovern had placed the weapon in the dash compartment of a bureau-owned Hudson. When he looked for it two days later, he discovered it missing. He immediately reported the matter to the Dayton police department.[47]

On June 24, Hoover sent McGovern a letter telling him he was being suspended from 9 a.m. June 26 until 9 a.m. June 29 for the loss of his weapon. McGovern had been in the Cincinnati office a little over a year, and he was not asked to resign, probably because of his length of service, age, and the hope he would gain maturity. It is well known that even senior agents have lost their bureau weapons. In today's bureau the loss of a weapon will generally get an agent suspended for the same amount of time—three days.[48]

The G-man and the Diamond King

ENDNOTES

* Definition of Bureau terms:

Special Agent (SA)— A federal criminal investigator with authority through Congress allowing investigative jurisdiction over violations in more than two hundred categories of federal law.

Inspector— Responsible for reviewing the investigative and administrative product of the FBI, at field offices and headquarters. Also conducts special investigations as directed.

Special Agent in Charge (SAC)— The head of each FBI office who leads the investigative mission and priorities.

Field Divisions— are composed of a field office and resident agencies (smaller satellite office). They conduct the federal criminal investigations to include national security matters (terrorism, counterintelligence, cyber) and background investigations.

Squad— The Special Agents at the field office level are organized into squads, which in the early FBI were supervised by the SAC.

The Investigator— The FBI in-house magazine published by employees and sponsored by the FBI Recreation Association. It began on April 4, 1932, from a suggestion from an employee. It is no longer published in softcover format but can be found on the FBI in-house website.

† As in the 1920s and 1930s, the FBI currently has a Performance Appraisal Review (PAR) completed for agents once per year with a mid-year progress report; file reviews are every ninety days, with First Office Agents having them every sixty days. The SAC position duties are to direct and manage investigative and intelligence gathering activities as directed by the FBI's top ten priorities. These are: 1. Protect the United States from terrorist attack, 2. Protect the United States against foreign intelligence operations and espionage, 3. Protect the United States against cyber-based attacks and high-technology crimes, 4. Combat public corruption at all levels, 5. Protect civil rights, 6. Combat transnational/

Nelson Klein, the original agent

national criminal organizations and enterprises, 7. Combat major white-collar crime, 8. Combat significant violent crime, 9. Support federal, state, local and international partners, 10. Upgrade technology to successfully perform the FBI's mission. The FBI's Supervisory Special Agent (SSA) conducts the file reviews and completes the PARs for agents under their supervision. SACs complete PARs for agents under their immediate supervision, which is usually a small number.

‡ James Egan was born around 1890 in Omaha, Nebraska, and joined the FBI in June of 1922. One of Hoover's "Big Five" during the mid-1930s when the Bureau was investigating gangs operating in the Midwest, Egan was promoted to inspector in 1927, and oversaw the internal accounting of the Bureau and the preparation of investigative accounting evidence for prosecution. He died in 1959. (*The FBI: A Comprehensive Reference Guide*, Edited by Athan G. Theoharis, 1999 Oryx Press, Phoenix, Arizona, 323.)

§ The FBI currently has in place an Office of preference list also known as Personnel Resource List (PRL) and Hardship Program (Medical, Child Custody and Financial). The list was established to provide agents a way to document a preferred office of assignment, which can be done in January and July of each year.

‖ William A. Rorer Sr. is known for his pivotal role in the apprehension of "Machine Gun" Kelly and the resulting term "G-Men" for the FBI. Bureau historian, Dr. John Fox, has noted at the FBI's website that the story of "Don't Shoot G-Men" is questionable at best and whether Kelly really said that at the time of his arrest has been a controversial subject. Rorer's son, Davis, however told Former Special Agent Larry Wack a few years back when he spoke to him by telephone that his father repeated the story to him and others many times over. Regardless, Rorer had a formative role in the early Bureau of the 1930's with many of the gangster investigations. He was born at Lynchburg, VA and was a veteran of World War I. After leaving the FBI, Rorer spent nearly thirty years in Albany and was president and general manager of Colonial Refrigeration at the time of his

The G-man and the Diamond King

death. (Reference source obit, Former Special Agent Larry Wack at *www.historicalgmensquarespace.com*.)

[#]Hugh H. Clegg was born in 1898 in Mathiston, Mississippi, and graduated in 1920 from Millsaps College, Jackson, Mississippi, with a bachelor of arts degree. He then attended George Washington University Law School and between 1922 and 1923 taught at Bennett Academy and Preparatory School in Mathiston, where he had attended. He entered duty with the FBI on August 12, 1926, and within a short period was designated an SAC assigned to offices in Atlanta, Washington, and Chicago. In 1932, he was made Assistant Director. He was also one of the first to hold the position of Inspector. By the time the "war on crime" hit America in the early 1930s, Hugh Clegg had already been in the Bureau over five years. (It was Clegg, not SAC Purvis, who was the ranking FBI official at the ill-fated shootout at the Little Bohemia Lodge in April of 1934.) He was involved in many Depression era gangster investigations and major incidents of the period. He was the first head of the FBI National Academy, formed in 1935, and Assistant Director of the Training and Inspection Division. He was influential in professionalizing police, new FBI agent and agent in-service training. Upon retirement from the FBI in 1954, he served as a special assistant to the president of the University of Mississippi. He retired from that post in 1969, and died on December 12, 1979. (Former Special Agent Larry Wack at *www.historicalgmensquarespace.com* & *The FBI: A Comprehensive Reference Guide*)

Barrett, like many of his
        neighbors and kinsmen, turned early
to the making of illegal whiskey.

3 Nemesis: George Barrett, mountain playboy

The year George W. Barrett was born is anyone's guess, which suggested to some that as far as George was concerned, deception was native. (When he later made national headlines, *Time* magazine revealed that the "W." in his name didn't stand for anything.) News articles, family records, and government records listed his date of birth as anywhere from 1881 to 1888. Army records, however, said February, 1887, confirmed by census records showing it as February 27, 1887.[1] (Interviewed by the FBI in 1935, he said it was February 28.) The sixth child of William R. and Nancy Jane Barrett's eleven,[2] he began life in a mountain cabin among the dark hills near Manchester, the largest town and county seat of Clay County, in the heavily wooded foothills of the Cumberland Mountains of southeast Kentucky. U.S. Census records for 1900 listed the population of the county as 15,364.

Barrett was a skinny kid who grew up with the smell of corn mash in his nostrils and early on learned to master the use of a Winchester rifle. He explored the hills near his home on Goose Creek Hollow, carrying his rifle in his hand or slung over his shoulder, "watching as much for revenue agents as for squirrels, as I was taught to shoot both on sight."[3] Barrett acquired six years of schooling, but he was apparently ruled less by education and more by survival of the fittest, a prevalent ethic in his mountain county.[4]

He became the blood enemy of the Stiver clan across the way, not because they had done anything to him but because, like his father, he had been taught to hate them.[5] He was always eager to talk firearms, feuds, violence, and hatred of the law, which existed among the shadier elements of his surroundings. His contempt for revenue agents was worn as a badge of honor among the hill people.

In 1899, the Barretts moved from Clay County to Jackson County, where they purchased a 175-acre farm on Brushy Mountain in an area called Old Orchard. Two years later, they moved again, this time to a 200-acre tract of land they bought for $400 on War Fork, off Station Camp River. Jackson County, at 10,561 people, was even less populated than Clay County.

As Barrett became of age, he got curious about the world beyond the mountains. He had no desire to marry and settle down to the hardships of living in a log cabin and growing a few acres of tobacco and corn. He wanted a flashy way of life, and he learned from his sister that if he wanted to be popular with women, he couldn't use the rough language of the average mountain man. He dreamed of beautiful women, remembering his sister's advice as he carried on various affairs, of which he had more than his share. By the time he was 19, he was a real mountain playboy—by the estimation of others, as well as his own.[6]

He wanted to see the world outside Jackson County, and so in April of 1906, he enlisted with the U.S. Army, 87th Coastal Artillery at Cincinnati, Ohio. After about a year he returned to Jackson County "to strut before the home-folks in my uniform," he said in an interview, but to his disappointment, he received no heroes' welcome.[7]

George Barrett, circa 1907, made a handsome young soldier.

So in the late summer of 1908, he tried again, reenlisting in the 15th Infantry, Company M, at Columbus, Ohio. If he didn't get a parade, he did get something else suitable for a man whose line of work would soon be lawlessness and crime: he became a qualified marksman. He utilized every spare minute practicing with pistol and rifle. He boasted of being a dead shot and being able to kill a running coyote at three hundred yards, and he practiced "fanning a revolver and could do it with the deadly accuracy of an old-time Westerner." He'd been considered a good shot in the mountain country near his home, and now he was determined to be the best shot in the Army.[8][9]

MARRIAGES, AN ASIDE

Barrett's first marriage, in February of 1904 to Mobie Robinson of Irwine, Kentucky, lasted only three months before a divorce in May of the same year. In 1910, after he had reenlisted in the Army and was serving as a private at Fort Douglas, Utah, he married Mary Alice Jones at Salt Lake City, and the following year they had a son—Delbert Lavoy Barrett. Barrett served his full three-year enlistment, was discharged in the late summer of 1911, and went to work for the Salt Lake City Water Works Department.

Soon, however, Barrett's second marriage paled, and he ended up once more in divorce court. In September of 1913, he married Agnes Durbin back in Lee County, Kentucky, but had no better marital luck than before. Agnes was soon gone, the relationship's only testimony being a daughter, Velma Lucille. Ever the hopeful aspirant, Barrett, in March of 1916, married a fourth time. She was Mattie T. McQueen of Irvin, Kentucky, although the dust hadn't settled from Barrett's third marriage: the divorce wasn't finalized. A son, Carlos, was born before George and Mattie called it quits in 1922.

Before divorce number four, though, Barrett had wooed a *fifth* woman and in the spring of 1918, a third son arrived. By this time, Barrett's marital math was such that his wives seemed to have only given names. Census records showed that Barrett married a woman named Lizzie in Missouri and another named Eunice in Hamilton, Ohio. Eunice apparently bore him a son, Jack Dempsey Barrett, in 1923 before she, in an odd role reversal for the Barrett marital chronicles, left *him*, taking off to New York City with a butcher from Carthage, Ohio.

Having seemingly exhausted wives in several states, Barrett returned to the scene of an earlier marital crime, and on the day before Thanksgiving in 1929 he remarried Alice Jones. Alice had remarried after her own divorce from Barrett and was now a widow with three children of her own. True to form, Barrett soon moved on: in the fall of 1931, he was keeping company with Sally Johnson, daughter of his double first cousin, and in the spring of 1938, Barrett had another daughter, Dolores. A marriage license was obtained in Lexington, Kentucky, but there was no record of a ceremony.

After Dolores was born, Barrett performed what was probably the most commendable act of his entire life: he submitted himself voluntarily to a sterilization procedure. Then in the summer of 1933—when at last he could do no more harm—he separated from Sally.

Nemesis: George Barrett, mountain playboy

HIS WORKING LIFE

After the army, Barrett returned to Kentucky with the idea of relaxing awhile, then moving on to some easy racket. The making and selling of illegal whiskey was lucrative in 1911, so he jumped back into the business. During this time, a pretty girl lived with him as his common-law wife. The girl and his sister Sylvania dressed well and, according to Barrett, at least, they were the envy of the other hill women.[10]

By 1913, Barrett had become a member of a mountain gang that dealt in the distilling and selling of bootleg whiskey. According to Barrett, he had the local authorities in the palm of his hand. Unbeknownst to Barrett, though, he wasn't dealing just with the locals: Internal Revenue agents obtained evidence that he was selling liquor without a license, and they got a warrant for his arrest. Barrett paid no attention except to announce with his usual braggadocio that he would shoot on sight anyone that came for him.

On the afternoon of April 15, 1913, he and his younger sister Rachel were making a batch of whiskey at Clifton Mills in Breckenridge County. Barrett looked out of the old mill shed and saw a marshal coming down the path. Barrett stepped outside with his Winchester in hand and shouted a warning. The lawman, Deputy U.S. Marshal C.T. Nichols, yelled to Barrett that he was under arrest.

Barrett put the Winchester to his shoulder, but before he could pull the trigger he was hit by "a withering blast" from Nichols's sawed-off shotgun. Barrett's rifle went off and dropped to the ground. He grabbed his forearm where he had been hit and moaned he was dying. Rachel, meanwhile, leaped to snatch the gun from Barrett's hand. A deputy sheriff, who had entered the shed from the other direction, leaped upon Rachel and grabbed her arms. Barrett was badly wounded from the shotgun charge, but Rachel fought until she was finally subdued and handcuffed.[11 12 13]

Barrett was dragged off to jail in Louisville, where he was charged with the sale of liquor without a license. He pled guilty to the violation and was sentenced to thirty days at the Jefferson County Jail in Louisville, and a $100 fine. He was also indicted on willfully obstructing, resisting and opposing a United States marshal in the performance of his duty. The attorney made a motion to have the indictment filed away with the possibility to reinstate at a later date if needed. No lesson was learned by Barrett, and in his own words, he "came out of prison a wiser and more cunning criminal than I had gone in."[14 15]

His prospects in moonshine having gone dry, he served another stint in the army, and looked about for new interests. He moved into a much more profitable trade:

The G-man and the Diamond King

the fencing of stolen jewelry and supplying guns to organized crime. At first, he sold only watches and rings, then he became a diamond merchant, often carrying around a dozen or more expensive stones. He also carried a large amount of cash, usually around $1,000, which he liked to flash, hinting that it had been gained by less-than-honest means.[16]

Always the rogue, and mindful of his flamboyant lifestyle, he was continuously looking for a more profitable criminal activity. He developed a scam whereby he would go into a jewelry store and ask for the most expensive ring, and after pulling a large wade of bills from his pocket, would pay cash for the ring. He would then take the ring home, remove the stone, and replace it with one of inferior quality. He would return to the store, put on an act of outrage; accuse the store clerk of cheating him, and demand a refund. More times than not, these scams turned in his favor. [17] [18] [19]

One of Barrett's cousins, A.J. Barrett, told a story of Barrett coming to his house in Rockcastle County, wanting to sell A.J. a watch. It was gold with a lot of jewels and worth more than A.J. could afford. Barrett said he would sell it to him for $10, or that A.J. could win it. Barrett had him mark off a hundred feet from a tree, then hang the watch on a limb. A slight breeze was moving the watch enough to make it a difficult target. A.J said he didn't have the $10, but his father said he would cover it— George Barrett would never hit that small, moving target. Barrett pulled out his revolver, aimed, and blew the watch into pieces. It was plain to everyone that Barrett had come to show off. And his demonstration was worth a gold watch.[20]

Just after WWI, Barrett began selling rare guns and hot jewelry in and around St. Louis, Missouri. One of his more profitable deals was a diamond allegedly worth ten thousand dollars, which he bought and sold twice, clearing a sizable profit of twenty-seven hundred dollars.[21] [22]

According to Barrett, life in the 1920s was, indeed, roaring. "Everyone had plenty of money," he said. "Hot Jewelry and guns sold faster than I could get them. Long ago I had forgotten my pretty common-law wife, and after I returned home I carried on an affair with a nineteen-year-old girl. I married and divorced a red-headed girl at Urban, Kentucky, while I was carrying on affairs with three other women."[23]

In the fall of 1924, Barrett sold illegal firearms near Urbana, Homestead, and Findlay, Missouri. Sheriff Fillmore McKenzie caught Barrett at a hotel in Homestead with an underage girl, possibly age 14. His room was searched and a quantity of stolen firearms and jewelry were found. He was charged with carrying a concealed weapon and violating immorality laws and fined one hundred and eighty dollars.[24]

Still a young man, this mugshot captures a more menacing Barrett.

In August of 1928, Barrett was back from his sojourn west. Marion Brewer, Barrett's brother-in-law by one of his common-law marriages, went to see Barrett and told him to send his sister some money as she was having a rough time financially. Barrett and Brewer had words and Barrett reached for his gun, but despite previous assertions that he could beat anyone to the draw, he did not. Birdshot from Brewer's shotgun hit him in his left eye. As a result, he lost his left eye and started wearing glasses, which made him look more dignified, like a businessman, professor, or preacher. Brewer and Barrett supposedly settled their quarrel without involving the sheriff.[25]

The eye was removed at Bethesda Hospital in Cincinnati and replaced with a glass eye, and at some time thereabouts, Barrett was living on Vine Street, working as a Cincinnati streetcar conductor, on the Lockland line. Of course, he found other advantages to his position, and—being a conductor—he began to conduct fencing operations on his streetcar, at cut-rate prices. Lockland police evidently knew about him, indicating that he was well-liked by his co-workers and even going so far as to say he was "a nice guy."[26]

In September of 1930, Barrett was visiting his sister, Rachel Maupin, and his 73-year-old mother, at their cabin in Jackson County's Clover Bottom. At about 8:30 a.m., Barrett returned from a trip from the general store and found his eleven-year-old son, Jack, crying at the gate. Barrett went up the path to the cabin and found his mother at the stove preparing supper. He asked her why she had given Jack a spanking, and she said, "That boy is just like yourself: mean and nasty. He tried to beat the dog with a whip." Barrett's first response was to punch his mother in the mouth, whereupon she picked up a broom and hit him on the arm.[27 28 29]

The G-man and the Diamond King

Barrett's second response was to shoot her in the stomach with his .38 revolver. When she followed him into the yard, he shot her twice more—once in her chest and again in her mouth. She died two hours later. Barrett returned to the cabin, washed, dressed, and went to his car. When his sister tried to stop him, he shot her, too, and pistol-whipped her. She managed to flee onto the state road and flag down the mail car, and Barrett shot at it with his Winchester, managing to somehow miss both the driver and Rachel.[30] She reached the hospital at McKee, Kentucky, where she spent six weeks but never fully recovered from her wounds, finally succumbing to pneumonia. She was only 36.

Barrett's brothers, John and Gilbert, were working in the nearby fields and heard the gunfire. When they reached the house, Barrett said he'd killed their mother and he'd kill them, too, if they tried to stop him. They told police Barrett had returned with his son from Idaho about six months previously to visit relatives in the vicinity of Big Hill

George Barrett's mother, Nancy Bolin Barrett, known as "Old Nance of the hills."

and Clover Bottom. He hadn't been in the area for more than sixteen years. The family, by this time, had become well-off and prominent in Clover Bottom. [31]

They said Barrett was unemployed, the black sheep of the family, and he'd caused the family numerous problems over the years, his father paying thousands of dollars to get him out of jams. He gave the appearance of being wealthy, however, wearing diamonds and spending large amounts of money. There were rumors he'd been seen in Berea, Kentucky, with a sack full of diamonds that must have been worth $25,000. No one knew where—or how—Barrett had obtained the diamonds.[32] [33]

Barrett was thought to be carrying four pistols and a high-powered .270 Winchester rifle, and a posse composed of Sheriff Albert Bogie and Deputy Lloyd Lane, of Madison County, and Sheriff Joe Pence and Deputy Leonard Abney of Jackson County, were searching for Barrett. The police were told that Barrett had a bank account with the

Berea National Bank, and an officer was assigned to surveillance there in case Barrett showed up.[34]

Barrett's brother, John, told Policeman E.T. Hays and Sheriff Bogie to shoot Barrett on sight if they found him. Flem Davis Sampson, the governor of Kentucky, offered a state reward of $200, the Barretts offered $250, and the county $250, making the reward for Barrett's capture and conviction $700. Rumors placed him in various locations across Kentucky but Barrett had fled west, ultimately to Cheyenne, Wyoming, where he reunited with his wife at the time.[35] The wanted posters described Barrett as "partially bald with gray hair, 5-foot-9, 175 pounds, glass eye, neat dresser, good talker, pleasant personality, with the appearance of a businessman."[36]

HIS FIRST MURDER TRIAL

In 1930, Frank H. Baker—Barrett's cousin—was elected Commonwealth Attorney for Clay County, Kentucky. In early September, Baker obtained an indictment against Barrett for the murder of Barrett's mother. In April of 1931, Barrett decided to give up the life of a fugitive and returned to Kentucky to face the murder charge against him. He spent a week in the Jackson County Jail and was released on bail. [37 38 39]

On his mother's side of the family, Barrett was a Baker, and he usually described his early childhood hatreds by explaining the Barrett-Stivers feud. Another of Barrett's relatives, W.T. McHone, author of *The Barrett Family of Clay County Kentucky and Collateral Families*, could find no information corroborating this feud. Frank Baker, however, was involved with the Baker-Howard feud, and Barrett made a deal with Baker: if Baker conducted a weak prosecution during his murder trial, he, Barrett, would become Baker's bodyguard for the duration of his term in office. [40]

The case came to trial on January 12, 1932. Barrett's defense was that he acted in self-defense, as his mother and sister had deliberately beat his son to get him angry so they could kill him. Barrett gave an award-winning performance on the stand, even at one point resorting to tears when he talked about his young son.[41] The

The Jackson County jail was one of Barrett's early lodging places; in 1931, he spent a week here.

The G-man and the Diamond King

prosecution's evidence was meager at best, even though the eye-witness testimony of Mabel Barrett—wife of Gilbert Barrett, Barrett's brother—was substantial and read as follows:

"George went runnin' toward the house with his shotgun in his hand. Then the shots came crashin' and Ma and Rachel staggered from the house. George fired three more times at Ma's head and she fell almost at his feet. Then Rachel hit him with an ax. He turned the gun on her and when it was empty started to beat her over the head with the barrel. She run staggerin' toward the road and hopped on the mail truck that was just passin'. George run out to his car and grabbed his Winchester and emptied it into the mail truck." [42]

After Barrett's testimony, Commonwealth Attorney Baker rose and said, "If the court pleases, the people move to dismiss the indictment on the grounds of insufficient evidence."

The circuit judge banged down his gavel and said, "Motion denied." (He would later remark that Baker the prosecutor sounded more like Baker the defense attorney.) The circus continued, with both defense and prosecution arguing for acquittal. The jury was bewildered and unable to reach a verdict. [43]

In early September of 1932, Barrett went to trial—again—for the murder of his mother, and it was a repeat of the first trial, a setup. The jury was unable to reach a verdict. The circuit judge placed in the record the following: "The defendant is charged with killing his mother who, at the time of her death, was a very old and feeble woman. Without going into the details of the trial, it is sufficient to say that, when the evidence was all in, the jury instructed, and the defense counsel had argued the case at length for the defendant, the Commonwealth Attorney, who writes on this indictment and moves to dismiss the case, made an open argument to the jury for the defendant, urged it to acquit the defendant, and said that it ought to do so, and still the jury hung." [44]

Barrett walked out of the courtroom a free man, never to be tried again on the charge of his mother's murder. He bragged that it cost him $1,700 to bribe two of his relatives to lie on the witness stand and said, "Didn't I tell you money will get you out of anything?" [45]

THE BAKER-HOWARD FEUD

Feud is defined by the dictionaries as "a mutual enmity or quarrel that is often prolonged or inveterate." The Baker-Howard feud was of a shorter duration then the other Kentucky feuds (Hatfield & McCoy), lasting from the beginning of the nineteenth century to the early twentieth century. In 1806, a hunting party looking for elk turned to cattle-stealing and the result was the cattle wars. The names of the casualties from both sides were listed as somewhere between fifty-five to 150. [46]

"In the years leading to the Civil War three homicides, which resulted in two hangings and one acquittal, caused the Baker-Howard separation," wrote Keith Otterbein in *American Anthropologist*. "These Clay County, Kentucky, residents all fought for the north in the Civil War. In the latter part of the nineteenth century a strain rose over the sale of timber. The leaders of both factions, Baldy George Baker and Big Jim Howard, worked out the differences, but the agreement did not reach some factions on both sides. The next day there was an ambush, and two of the Howards were killed and one was wounded. On April 19, 1898, Big Jim Howard shot Baldy George Baker, which resulted in his death. A series of payback killings resulted. On June 10, 1899, Tom Baker was shot and killed while in protective custody of the Kentucky State militia. The feud lingered in the 1930s, with three Bakers being killed in two ambushes, possibly by Howards, including Jim." [47]

Not long after the trial, Baker's work as attorney took a turn into complexity. A grand jury had indicted Dewey Hensley, Little Tom Baker, and Frank McDaniel for burning a warehouse where Alf Neal had been killed, and Baker had refused to continue with the legal process against the men. The Howards from the Baker-Howard feud were demanding that Baker prosecute these cases. The Bakers, for their part, were demanding that Baker take a second look at old cases against the Howards and Whites for the killing of the Bakers. The strain of being in the middle was starting to show on Baker and he confided to his mother that he had a premonition that he wasn't long for the world. [48]

At the time, Baker was counsel in a civil case in Clay County, and the following morning was to go to the courthouse at Manchester for a hearing. Because the case would take at least a week to try, he rented quarters for himself and his three bodyguards at the Potter Hotel across the street from the courthouse. Each day, he crossed with his bodyguards—John Brockman, another cousin, and George Barrett, who had agreed to assist as Baker was expecting trouble.

They left the hotel and got to the middle of the street when three men with rifles started shooting at them from the courthouse. Baker and Brockman were killed, and Barrett rolled under his own vehicle and was not injured. His car was found to have sixteen bullet holes in it. A few minutes later, an answering volley of gunfire came from the cliffs on the other side of Goose Creek. The shooting didn't end until two o'clock in the afternoon. Sheriff's deputies, who were riding on the running boards of Barrett's car with shotguns, escorted Barrett to Burning Springs on U.S. 421 and told him to never return. A detachment of state militia arrived in Manchester to keep the peace. [49]

No one knows who killed Frank Baker. Most likely it was a Howard family member. Baker's body lay on the sidewalk for hours; everyone in the hotel, including his mother,

The G-man and the Diamond King

was afraid to remove it. By the time the body was retrieved, the enemy had moved on. The Baker family believed that the bullets which killed Baker came from the rifle of Big Jim Howard, even though his grandson said it was not his style to not face his enemy.[50] On January 24, 1934, an indictment was issued charging Tolman Burchill, James Stivers, Tolman Stivers, and John Burchill with the murder of Frank Baker.

In June of 1934, Barrett was still trying to work the system. On June 20, he was indicted for grand larceny in Hardinsburg in Breckinridge County. Apparently, Barrett had stolen a suitcase from a local hotel, although the charges were reduced to conversion of personal property, taking another's property without consent, and he was fined $100. On June 28, he registered himself and an underage girl, Edna Parrott, at the Grand Hotel in Hazard as J.D. Long and wife. On June 29, the Hazard police judge issued an arrest warrant for Barrett, charging him with selling pistols without a license. On the same day, Barrett was arrested for being in possession of nine pistols of different makes. And there was more—he and Edna Parrott were arrested and charged with adultery. They were fined $20 and costs and Edna, who was from Grey Hawk in Jackson County, stayed at the sheriff's residence until her father came for her.[51]

Edna's mother, Mrs. Will Parrott, was interviewed by the FBI in 1935 and said that Barrett had dated Edna for some time. Barrett had obtained a marriage certificate, which said that Barrett and Edna had been married at Newport, Kentucky in January of 1934, but Edna claimed he had forged it. Mrs. Parrott said that Barrett was a bad man and often drove new cars when he called at her home. He also seemed to have plenty of money, carrying around over $1,000. And Barrett often said that he would never go willingly to the penitentiary. He would use his money to get out of it, or he would kill himself.[52]

There was another option for the career criminal George Barrett, but it is difficult to think he planned for it. And while this choice would serve to elevate him out of the ranks of ordinary hoodlums, it also took him to a place in which his down-home charm—or even his money—wouldn't help him.

The Kansas City shootout in 1933
would make agents everywhere nervous.

The Cincinnati office eyes Barrett

For at least four years Barrett—aka George W. Ball, James L. Black, George W. Martin, James L. Anderson, George H. Clark, J.D. Long, J.D. Little, George Smith, and White Burnett— had been suspected by the FBI as a violator of the National Motor Vehicle Theft Act.[1] He began dealing in stolen automobiles in 1931. His method was to buy an automobile, obtain title papers for it, steal an automobile of similar description, change its motor numbers to correspond with those on the purchase car, obtain duplicate title papers, then sell the stolen car to a dealer. In 1935, he was living in Hamilton, Ohio, where his brother, Gilbert, had a home. At the time, Gilbert was serving a prison sentence at the Indiana State Penitentiary in Michigan City.

The Cincinnati FBI office was investigating Barrett under Bureau file 26-2816,* which was titled "Charles W. Woods, alias Charles Martin; George Barrett, alias George W. Martin; William Lee Cromer; National Motor Vehicle Theft Act (NMVTA)." The file showed that Barrett, using the alias George W. Martin, rented an automobile from the Dixie Drive It Yourself Company in Birmingham, Alabama, on October 1, 1931. The car was later found in the possession of two men named Woods and Cromer, at Lockland, Ohio, where they were arrested in November of 1931 on suspicion of burglary and carrying firearms.

It seemed likely that the men had either helped Barrett steal the car or bought it from him and knew it was stolen. It also appeared that Barrett borrowed the names of confederates from time to time and used them as his aliases. The file said Barrett was involved in dealing with stolen cars, stolen jewelry, possibly bank robbery, and that he had killed his mother and sister. Another file entry said Barrett was also the central figure in an insurance fraud case being investigated by the General Exchange Insurance Company.

On August 1, 1935, Agent Donald C. McGovern of the Cincinnati FBI Office went to the police department in Covington, Kentucky, to talk to Detectives John Dress and James D. Higgins. He, along with the two detectives, then went to see Milton E. Tritsch, a Covington locksmith, where they learned that Barrett had visited the locksmith on a number of occasions over the previous five months, having keys made for various automobiles. McGovern got a description of Barrett, the car he was driving, and its license plate number.[2]

Tritsch said it was possible to secure key numbers for 1935 automobiles in only two ways—one from the owner, the other from the dealer who sold the vehicle. Someone acting in a nefarious manner could ascertain owner names and the name of the dealer, contact the dealer to get the key number, then use this to get a duplicate key. Barrett got his duplicates by having the key number in advance.

On August 14, McGovern drove to College Corner (also known as West College Corner), Indiana, where he learned that Barrett had another brother, John D. Barrett, who lived in the town. The postmaster told McGovern that George Barrett lived with his brother, and the brother's children sometimes picked up mail at the post office addressed to George W. Ball. The postmaster also showed McGovern where John Barrett lived.[3]

McGovern left College Corner and went to Hamilton, Ohio, where he interviewed Scott Finlay, manager of the Central Motors Company on North Second Street. McGovern had previously seen FBI files that showed Barrett having business dealings with Central Motors. In the Finlay interview, McGovern learned that in the middle of July, 1935, Barrett had ordered a new 1935 black Chevrolet coupe with tree bark upholstery. He paid for it on July 31 and received his title.

Finlay, the manager at Central Motors, apparently had a head for numbers, as he'd previously worked for a finance company. When the paperwork came in covering a transaction on the type of car Central sold, it caught his eye. Finlay went through the paperwork and determined that the car had been sold by a used car dealer in Hamilton, Arthur Hock, to a Reverend Thomas Farmer. The Farmer car had the same motor number as the car Finlay had sold to Barrett. The car that was sold to Barrett was the special order that Barrett waited two weeks for, the 1935 black Chevrolet coupe with tree bark upholstery.

Finlay thought it strange that this car had been sold by Barrett so soon after he purchased it, and he told the agents that Barrett had always been a puzzle to him. Barrett always had a roll of cash, and sometimes diamonds, and while Finlay didn't know exactly what Barrett's racket was, he was fairly certain it wasn't legal.[4]

When McGovern interviewed Arthur Hock, he learned Hock had sold Thomas Farmer the used automobile which Hock had purchased from Barrett on the morning of August 2.

The G-man and the Diamond King

Barrett had delivered to Arthur Hock a used Chevrolet, similar in description and bearing the identical motor number as the new car Barrett had just bought from Central Motors.[5]

It was clear to the agents that Barrett was a professional car thief using the so-called "Mother System," that is, stealing a car, having a false bill of sale made, then changing the serial numbers on the car to match the bill of sale (this meant, of course, that there could be several makes of the same car out there somewhere, all with identical serial numbers and bills of sale). Barrett had stolen the Farmer car, bought a new one to match it, changed the motor number of the stolen car to agree with the legitimately purchased car, then sold the stolen car using his title papers from the legitimate car.

On the morning of August 15, McGovern continued the Barrett investigation by interviewing police officers in Lockland. Chief Andrew Wagner of the Lockland Police Department had received a letter dated December 19, 1934, from the San Diego Police Department about the theft of a Chevrolet from Hertz-Drive-Ur-Self in San Diego. A grand theft warrant for Barrett had been issued in San Diego. McGovern returned to the Cincinnati FBI office, explaining to Acting SAC Howard Harris and Agent Klein everything he knew about Barrett.[6]

That afternoon, McGovern and Harris went to Hamilton and interviewed Thomas Farmer. When they examined his automobile, they found the numbers had been changed: they were identical to the motor numbers on the car Hock had bought from Barrett on August 27.[7]

There was no doubt that George Barrett was a bad man, but the full extent of his badness was not yet known—although shooting his own mother was a good indicator. In the early 1930s, he was what the newspapers called "a rather nasty but ordinary enough career criminal."[8] That was about to change, though, and what happened next came against a national backdrop in which the criminal element seemed to hold sway against the forces of law enforcement.

AGENTS AND THEIR GUNS

In the 1930s, BOI agent-training was in its infancy; they were undermanned and out-gunned. In 1930, there were twenty-five field offices across the country and some four hundred agents.[9] As a point of comparison, the city of Chicago alone had more than a thousand gangs by the mid-1920s.[10] Criminals had more money to buy weapons (either legally or illegally)—consider, for a moment, all the ill-gotten gains from bootlegging— and they had the added advantage of being able to steal what they wanted. When criminals began to use the Thompson submachine gun, it seemed that they'd acquired most of them by exactly that—stealing them. To add real injury to insult, a lot of them came from the police departments themselves, because the smaller departments with perhaps a single officer on midnight duty made easy targets. Security was not much better at National Guard Armories, another easy target.[11]

The Thompson, by this time, had become the era's icon. If an enterprising criminal hadn't heisted one, he might buy one in a hardware store, although it's unlikely many hardware stores stocked an item so expensive—$175 to $225, which would be more than $3,000 in today's dollars.[12] The hoodlums of the day had another advantage: Ford's new flathead V-8 in 1932 made a great getaway car.[13] At its outset, it was said to be able to outrun the police cars. John Dillinger used its running boards as "mobile platforms for machine-gunning henchmen,"[14] and Clyde Barrow wrote Henry Ford his personal thanks: "Dear Sir: While I still have got breath in my lungs I will tell you what a dandy car you make. I have drove Fords exclusively when I could get away with one. For sustained speed and freedom from trouble the Ford has got it over ever other car skinned and even if my business hasen't been strickly legal it don't hurt anything to tell you what a fine car you got in the V8…"[15]

Then came the defining moment—an event known as the Kansas City Massacre. In July of 1933, law enforcement agents and their prisoner, Frank "Jelly" Nash, a notorious bank robber, got off a train in Union Station, to take Nash to Leavenworth Federal Penitentiary, just north of the city. They were ambushed by gunmen and four law enforcement agents died, along with Nash. The shootout was first thought to have been an attempt to rescue Nash, but there was also speculation that it was a mob assassination aimed at silencing him.

The BOI identified the assassins as Pretty Boy Floyd, Adam Richetti, and Verne Miller, who'd been a WWI hero. The historical record, however, was never completely clear about that, either. Several biographers wrote that the massacre wasn't in Floyd's style, that he was merely a handy scapegoat. Even Floyd himself—who was killed the next year in an Ohio gunfight—sent a postcard to the Kansas City police denying it.[1]

Theories abounded, but one thing was certain: the Kansas City Massacre helped make J. Edgar Hoover and his fledgling organization. First, there was a great outcry by the public, where sentiment was beginning to shift from the Depression romance in which thieves and killers were seen as glamorous anti-authority figures. Now, the public was becoming aware of the real dangers. Second, Hoover skillfully used the incident to expand the scope and authority of the BOI.

The G-man and the Diamond King

The Pretty Boy

He was a poor-boy legend in Oklahoma where the folks there considered him a nervy desperado taking revenge on Depression era fat cat bankers. When he robbed banks, the legend went, he destroyed the mortgage documents, freeing the locals of their debts. Oklahoma people protected him—and the legend—calling him "the Robin Hood of Cookson Hills."[17] He was first arrested as a teenager for stealing $3.50 in coins from a post office, but soon he'd moved up. After one heist, the victim described Floyd as "a mere boy — a pretty boy with apple cheeks." Another account said the name was given to him by a prostitute. Wherever it came from, Floyd hated it.[18] He robbed banks in Missouri and Ohio, got caught in Ohio, and on his way to prison escaped by jumping off the train. He was thought to have killed several men, including a federal agent, and after the death of John Dillinger, Floyd graduated to Public Enemy Number One. His notoriety reached its apex with the Kansas City Massacre in 1933 when four law enforcement agents were killed, and he died the next year in a shootout in an eastern Ohio cornfield where he'd been cornered by Melvin Purvis and a squad of his agents and some East Liverpool, Ohio, policemen.[19] The body went back to Oklahoma where his funeral was attended by a crowd estimated as large as 40,000—the largest funeral in the state's history.[20]

◆ For the largest funeral ever held in Oklahoma, Charles Arthur Floyd left a handsome corpse.

The next year, in 1934, Congress enacted legislation giving DOJ Agents the power of arrest and the authority to carry firearms—the first federal gun-control legislation. Previously, agents could only make a "citizen's arrest." Otherwise, the agent had to call on a U.S. marshal or local police officer to take custody of a suspect. The new law expanded agency authority, and it created more uniformity of laws across various jurisdictions. After 1934, for instance, it was a federal crime to rob a national bank, and the law soon covered bank burglary, larceny, and other such crimes.[21]

The Bureau, of course, issued—and agents carried—weapons long before the law was passed in 1934, although this fact was not routinely known. In a 1955 letter to the *Grapevine*,[†] agent Roy McHenry said when he received his Bureau badge in 1917, he was also issued a Smith & Wesson automatic handgun. (Bureau training manuals of 1929 said agents were allowed to carry and use weapons, although "for defensive purposes only.")[22] There were even a few submachine guns in the agency, too. Hoover even allowed his men to buy their own although at an agent's salary of $2,800, not many could afford one.[23]

Many thought the Kansas City Massacre was also the formative moment for the Bureau creating its academy and formal weapons training. Field offices now kept special equipment for agents: Colt monitor automatic rifles, automatic shotguns, high-powered rifles, machine guns, gas riot guns, gas grenades, protective shields, and bulletproof vests.[24]

Agent Klein, who had begun his career with little or no training, was being brought up to date. A memorandum in Klein's personnel file, written by Cincinnati SAC Earl Connelley and dated April 3, 1934, said that Klein had qualified with a handgun at target practice from fifteen and twenty-five yards in November and December of 1933, and January, February, and March of 1934. He received more firearms training each month in the first quarter of 1935.

In 1929, Colt introduced a variant to the M1911—the M1911A1, the Colt .38 super automatic pistol issued to Klein. The M1911 had established a reputation with the military, police, and the general public. The Super .38 had a magazine capacity of nine, so with one in the chamber it was possible to have ten rounds available. The barrel was five inches long with fixed sights, weighed thirty-nine ounces, with an overall length of eight-and-a-half inches.

The weapon's ability to penetrate body armor and automobile bodies was well known by criminals. When the Super .38 was introduced, it was considered the most powerful automatic pistol in the world. John Dillinger and Baby Face Nelson had a

The G-man and the Diamond King

Texas gunsmith convert Colt pistols to fully automatic submachine guns with extended magazines and Thompson submachine gun foregrips. Texas Rangers, FBI Agents, and sheriffs all started carrying the Colt. Even Hoover had a Colt Super .38. [25]

This Colt Super .38 Automatic is the same gun used by Agent Klein.

Both Klein and Barrett had gained proficiency with firearms during military training, each received marksmanship honors, and each had kept more than a passing familiarity with their weapons.

Their skills as marksmen were about to receive the supreme test.

ENDNOTES

*Under the current FBI Investigative Classification a 26 matter is Interstate Transportation of Stolen Motor Vehicles (ITSMV).

†The Grapevine is the Society of Former Special Agents of the FBI internal magazine.

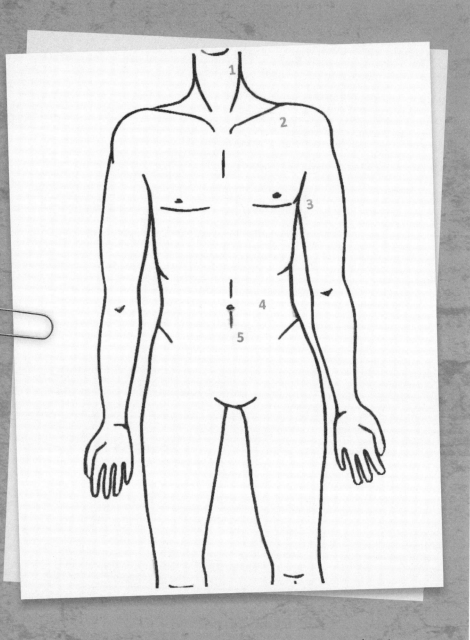

This diagram shows the location of Agent Klein's bullet wounds after the shooting.

The shootout: August 16, 1935

On the morning of August 16, Agent Klein was grooming his fingernails while waiting outside his residence for a ride from McGovern. He was always well dressed, and this day he was wearing a brown pinstriped three-piece suit, white shirt, conservative tie, and—of course—a fedora hat.

The two agents had previously obtained information from the Automobile Protective and Information Bureau in Chicago, verifying that the Farmer car had been stolen in St. Louis, Missouri. During the investigation, McGovern asked a number of people in Hamilton, Ohio, to contact him if Barrett appeared there. Around 10:30 a.m., Scott Finlay of Central Motors got word to the Cincinnati FBI office that Barrett was at Central Motors. Klein called the Hamilton Police Department and requested the chief arrest Barrett on the FBI's behalf. The agents tried to get a federal warrant for Barrett but were unable to do so because the U.S. Attorney's office had closed at 1 p.m.

In the early afternoon of August 16, Scott Findlay contacted Klein and said Barrett left the Central Motors lot before the police arrived. After a meeting with acting SAC Harris, Klein and McGovern were sent after Barrett—first to Hamilton, then to College Corner, Indiana—to arrest him for violation of the National Motor Vehicle Theft Act. The agents were unable to find Barrett in Hamilton, and they drove to College Corner, which was only about twenty miles west of Hamilton.[12]

They arrived in College Corner around 5:45 p.m. and immediately spotted, driving in front of them, a black Chevrolet coupe with 1935 Ohio license plates. They followed the vehicle as it turned onto Mound Street and parked near the mouth of an alley. The agents drove past the Chevrolet, watching two men get out of the car, one of whom—a large man in shirt sleeves—fit Barrett's description. The other male, they determined later, was Irvin Brockman. Klein and McGovern drove about two blocks to the end of Mound Street, turned around, and drove back in the direction they had just come. They passed the two men they had seen getting out of the parked Chevrolet, who were then walking down the sidewalk. [3][4]

The agents parked and McGovern got out and watched Barrett enter the front yard of a house where his brother, John D. Barrett, lived. McGovern went to where Barrett had parked his vehicle, examined the motor number, and saw it had not been changed— it was identical with the motor number of the new vehicle Barrett bought from Central Motors Company on August 2. (This meant that Barrett was driving the legitimate vehicle; it was Farmer's car which had the doctored numbers.)

McGovern returned to the bureau vehicle and briefed Klein on what he had learned. They were both convinced that the man they'd been following was George Barrett, and they intended to arrest him. They parked next to picnic grounds at the south end of Mound Street, in an attempt to blend into the neighborhood and still see Barrett's car. Klein went to a nearby house to find a telephone where he called the Butler County sheriff, requesting that two officers be sent to assist in the arrest of Barrett.[6][7][8]

The divided state of things

West College Corner, Indiana, is located about five miles northwest of Oxford, Ohio, mirrored by its Buckeye half, the village of College Corner, Ohio, and separated by the state line, which ran through the public school that served both places. This speck on the map became famous because its schoolhouse was the only one in America that occupied two states. When two players jumped for the ball at basketball tip-off, they'd each be in different states. "If, in late spring or early fall (Indiana did not then go on daylight saving time)," wrote *The New York Times*, "a player would put a desperation shot into the west basket from beyond midcourt, the ball would technically go through the hoop an hour before it left the shooter's hand...Logistical problems can also beget strange situations, like the one in 1978 when winter storms caused suspension of school for several days. Ohio's students were not permitted as many snow days as Indiana's, and so at the end of the year the Ohio pupils had to take a few field trips to the local park to meet state attendance requirements." [5]

The G-man and the Diamond King

♦ This 1935 sedan was the car driven by Agents McGovern and Klein.

Klein and McGovern waited in their car for the officers, just west of the intersection of Mound and Velocipede Street, when they saw Barrett walking east on Velocipede Street. Barrett kept walking and passed by the parked bureau vehicle in which Klein and McGovern were seated. The agents did not attempt to arrest Barrett when he walked past. They were waiting for arrest assistance from the sheriff's office, and they were somewhat concerned about attempting to arrest a dangerous criminal like Barrett without appropriate backup. [9] [10] [11]

A few minutes later, at approximately 6:30 p.m., the agents saw Barrett walking toward his vehicle. He was carrying something, which was later determined to be a hand towel stamped "Seibold Hotel"—and unbeknown to them, it was wrapped around a revolver. Barrett started to get into his car, which caused McGovern to start the bureau vehicle, thinking Barrett might flee. Barrett's car was parked near the mouth of an alley that ran perpendicular to the street where the agents were parked. McGovern drove the bureau vehicle toward Barrett. They could wait no longer for the sheriff's men; Barrett was leaving. Then he surprised them; he *didn't* leave. Instead, he got out of his car and began walking east down the alley.

McGovern drove past where Barrett's vehicle was parked, just opposite the entrance to the alley, and Klein jumped out of the car and yelled, "Just a minute, we're federal officers!" He was thirty or forty feet from Barrett, and the agent hadn't yet drawn his weapon. [12] [13] [14]

Barrett turned toward Klein, fumbled with something in front of his body, then turned back quickly, going farther down the alley. McGovern, meanwhile, hurriedly parked his vehicle, then jumped out to find his partner. About halfway down the alley was a garage, and as he ran, he heard shots fired from behind the garage. Then he heard Klein say, "Oh Lord, I'm shot!" [15] [16] [17]

The shootout: August 16, 1935

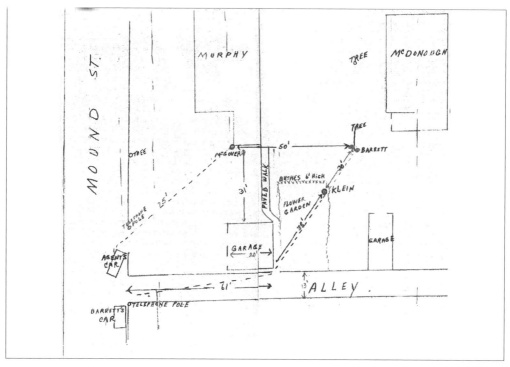

🔹 This drawing by Agent McGovern shows the alley where Klein pursued Barrett and died in the edge of a flower garden.

McGovern didn't continue down the alley; instead, he went around the garage on the Mound Street side, running in a northeastern direction in an attempt to get behind Barrett. He heard a rapid series of shots, and Klein said, "Oh Lord, I'm shot again!" McGovern took cover at the corner of a nearby house. [18] [19] [20]

From his vantage point, McGovern saw Barrett standing behind a tree, pointing his gun in McGovern's direction. McGovern shot at Barrett and hit him in the right leg, causing Barrett to fall behind the tree. McGovern shot only once. Barrett seemed seriously wounded and no longer a threat. [21] [22] [23]

Klein was lying about twenty-five feet from Barrett. McGovern ran to a nearby house to get medical help but couldn't reach either of the two College Corner doctors. When he returned, he found Klein lying on his side, hand outstretched in death and still grasping his gun. McGovern then tried to interview Barrett but Barrett, in considerable pain, could only tell McGovern his name and that he was from Kentucky. He asked for water and an ambulance. [24]

By this time, the Butler County sheriff had reached the scene, and McGovern asked him to accompany Barrett to the hospital, remaining in his custody until FBI agents could get there. [25]

The G-man and the Diamond King

Barrett regained his powers of speech at the hospital where he supposedly said, "I beat him to the draw! Sure, I shot him while he lay on the ground. It isn't the first time I've killed a man." [26]

The Union County coroner, Dr. W. L. Porter, arrived shortly afterward and released Klein's body, which was then taken by ambulance to Christ Hospital in Cincinnati where an autopsy was immediately performed by Dr. Porter and Dr. Douglas B. Remsen, the pathologist at Christ.

The agency's summary report read: "Five bullets entered the body of Klein, three of which had passed through and out of the body, and two of which were found lodged inside the body. One bullet (Bullet No. 1) entered the left side of the neck, severing the windpipe and affecting the jugular vein. This bullet passed out of the body and caused such a wound as would inevitably cause death. The place of entrance of this bullet was higher than the place of exit from the body. A second bullet entered Klein's body under the left shoulder, was traced through the bony process of the shoulder and found its exit from the body on the posterior edge of the shoulder and was not in the body. Yet another bullet (No. 3) entered on the arm and proceeded through the soft tissue of the large muscle in the back, from which it took exit and was not in the body. The fourth bullet entered in the lateral aspect of the abdominal region, penetrated the body of the vertebrae and lodged in the soft tissues just to the right of the spine, its course being slightly downward from the left side to the right, tearing the intestines and throwing contents of the intestines and blood into the abdominal cavity. This bullet destroyed the fifth vertebrae. Bullet No. 5 entered Klein's body in the inch or two below the umbilicus in the center of the abdominal region, the course of the bullet being downward from the left to the right, causing further tears in the intestines and the small vessels which lead to the intestines, shattering a portion of the pelvic bone and lodging in the thick part of the thigh. The two bullets removed from Klein's body by Dr. Remsen at the autopsy were introduced in evidence as

Agent McGovern makes headlines in his hometown.

exhibit number one. The death of Agent Klein resulted from hemorrhage and shock, secondary to gunshot wounds, and was caused by the entrance into Klein's body of one or more of these bullets." [27] [28] [29]

Barrett was examined at Fort Hamilton Hospital on the same evening. The doctors found two bullet holes in each of Barrett's legs, below the knees. The entry and exit in each leg formed a horizontal line with the entry on the right side. McGovern shot at Barrett from Barrett's right, so the horizontal line suggested the four wounds were probably caused by one bullet. [30] There was some confusion, however. Barrett said that Klein shot him in the left leg and McGovern in the right, and while it was possible that Klein missed Barrett with all ten of his shots, it was difficult to believe.

Barrett owned a Colt Bisley* Model .45 single action revolver, which he used during the gunfight with Agent Klein. The weapon was blue-steeled with elk bone grips. The serial number on the weapon was #318989. In an FBI interview on August 21—and later while testifying at his trial—Barrett said that he obtained the rare elk bone-handled weapon in El Paso, Texas, and had seen only one other like it. [31]

Agent Charles B. Winstead of the FBI's El Paso office determined that Barrett bought the weapon on July 5 from Nemiel Jaffee, an employee of Barnett's Pawn Shop in El Paso.

The Colt .45 had black rubber handles, which Jaffee recalled changing to another set of black rubber grips, because one of the handles was chipped.

Jaffee said the man who bought the gun used the name "White" and said that he was stopping at a hotel in El Paso. The purchase took place around noon and the man said he was retired Army. White told Jaffee he was going to a hotel to buy a collection of pistols and other guns.

◆ This Colt .45 Single Action Bisley is the kind of gun Barrett used to shoot Klein.

Jaffee couldn't positively identify Barrett from a photograph, but he said he believed the photograph to be that of the same man that purchased the weapon. [32]

There was a historical note to the death of Agent Klein, little remarked on and surely of small consequence to Klein's widow and children. It came about this way: for some time, Director Hoover had been vexed by the confusion among various government agencies that were known as "Division of Investigation." He was particularly annoyed because the Department of the Interior had one, and its agents, Hoover complained,

The G-man and the Diamond King

didn't say that belonged to the Department of the Interior, implying, of course, they were riding on the coattails of his agents. In the public's mind, Hoover said, there was only one Division of Investigation, and it was *his*. [33]

In Hoover's own mind, his agency was set definitely apart, and he wanted everyone to know it. In August of 1934, Hoover had written the acting attorney general requesting a name change, the AG agreed and took the issue to Congress and on March 22, 1935, President Franklin Roosevelt signed an appropriation bill that made the agency "the Federal Bureau of Investigation." [34]

This meant—sadly—that Nelson Klein was the first Federal Bureau of Investigation agent killed in the line of duty.

There was another note, a sad and personal one. It occurred when Acting SAC Harris went to the Klein home in Southgate to notify Klein's widow of her husband's death. Harris's family went with him, including Harris's daughter, Terry, who at six and a half years old remembered the scene.

They drove across the river, she recalled, on that hot day in August, and the Klein children were outside playing. And what Terry remembered was that when the children were told, they seemed not to fully understand what had happened. One of them, most likely Barbara Ann, who was three, began to say in a sing-song voice, "My daddy's dead we'll get another daddy, My daddy's dead we'll get a new daddy…"

ENDNOTES

* In 1894 the Colt Bisley was produced as primarily a target pistol, named after the famous firing range in Bisley, England. The Bisley is different from other Colt revolvers of the period, as it has a longer grip, a wider hammer spur, and a wider trigger. The most common calibers were .32-20, .38-40, .45 Colt, .44-40, .41 Colt, and the British calibers .450 Eley and .455 Eley. Most Bisley standard model revolvers shipped to the United States were not used for target shooting but rather for self-defense because the grip and hammer were ideal for fast shooting. (Alder, Dennis Colt Single Action: From Patersons to Peacemakers. Edison, NJ: Chartwell Books. 2008 Pg. 218-219)

The MEANEST man I ever knew

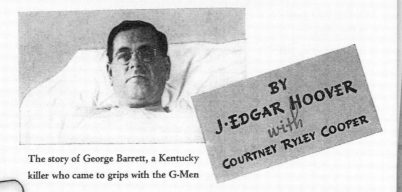

The story of George Barrett, a Kentucky killer who came to grips with the G-Men

BY J. EDGAR HOOVER with COURTNEY RYLEY COOPER

IT WAS in the deep afternoon of a summer day a year and a half ago that George Barrett walked into a room of his brother's home in the village of College Corners, Ohio, near the Indiana line, and opened the drawer of a dresser. A big man, heavily shouldered, tall, bespectacled, he was totally unlike the average man's conception of a desperado. His clothing was conservative. There was something of blandness about his expression, marred only by a lack of focus in one of his blue eyes. His hair, naturally iron-gray, was dyed brown.

Barrett's actions were those of a person who might be reaching into a drawer for a necktie or papers, anything except the well-oiled, blue-steeled, long-barreled revolver which lay there, wrapped in a hotel towel. He grasped the cloth-shielded weapon and, holding it close to him, started out of the house, only to be interrupted by his sister-in-law:

"Where are you going, George?"

"Oh," he answered easily. "I'm goin' to attend to a matter. Then I'll be seein' you." His tone was soft and unhurried, like that of a person born in Kentucky hills; there was no evidence of excitement.

Down the tree-lined street of the quiet town he walked until he reached his automobile, parked at the curb. There he stopped, looking furtively about him. Another car was approaching. The door opened. One of two men in the car leaped out.

"Just a minute, Barrett!" he said. "We're federal officers—"

GEORGE BARRETT whirled, ran zigzagging up an alley, and suddenly jumped behind a tree. The towel fluttered to the ground. Before Special Agent Nelson B. Klein could even reach for his automatic, a stream of fire burst from Barrett's weapon. Klein stumbled, went down. Barrett continued to fire as his victim fell, every bullet striking its mark. On the ground, mortally wounded, the special agent unholstered his automatic and returned the fire. A bullet struck the concealed Barrett in a knee which hardly protruded into view. The murderer winced, then fired two more shots into Klein's all but lifeless figure.

Then there came the sound of another shot. Klein's fellow officer was hurrying into the fight. A bullet struck Barrett in his unwounded leg. He staggered and again aimed, seeking to kill the second special agent. But the hammer fell harmlessly upon already exploded shells. He wavered and sank to the ground, a captive.

"I beat him to the draw!" he boasted later in the hospital. "Sure, I shot him while he lay on the ground. It isn't the first time I've killed a man."

The consequences of his act seemed to bother Barrett not at all. He had beaten other cases against him and it did not even enter his head that he might fail to beat this one. He had dodged the results of two other killings in which the weakest sort of plea had saved him. He had done everything from poisoning dogs to killing women without ever having even glimpsed the inside of a penitentiary. Through years of the weirdest sort of crimes, he had sneered at the law, thumbed his nose at Justice, and uttered the jeering boast that "nobody ever would bother" him.

However, Barrett had not considered one fact—that when a criminal shoots at a special agent of the Federal Bureau of Investigation he enters into a duel with a well-trained antagonist. Barrett killed his man from ambush; nevertheless, the marksmanship of the dying special agent and of a companion who came to his rescue was so expert that they were able to fell their adversary by hitting the tiny target formed by a part of his knees, exposed beside a tree behind which he had hidden.

Had Barrett escaped after this battle, he would have moved rapidly into the position of a major public enemy and become (Continued on page 137)

The Director **himself** gives Barrett national notoriety.

6 Aftermath: the bureau goes to work

Hoover did not wait for things to happen; he immediately went into high gear, using the public relations machine of the bureau. Just before 8 p.m., less than two hours after his agent had been killed, Hoover was on the telephone to the *Washington Herald*, the Associated Press, the night city editor of the *Washington Post*, and Universal News Service. He gave them the details surrounding the death of Agent Klein, and told each of them there was no provision under federal law to provide relief for the widows and children of agents killed in the line a duty. The FBI's own Employees Compensation Act,* which was made up of periodic $10 contributions by Special Agents, Hoover considered inadequate.[1]

In a memo dated August 26, 1935, prepared by W.R. Glavin† and addressed to Assistant Director Tolson, 414 Special Agents, including Klein and Director Hoover, contributed $10 to the Employees Compensation fund during 1935. This allowed for a check totaling $4,176.17 including $36.17 in interest to be provided to Mrs. Klein, upon her husband's death.

The day after Klein was killed, August 17, Crown Attorney Norman F. Newton of Ontario, Canada, provided a tribute to the agent in County Court. He had asked for and obtained a week remand in the cases of three kidnappers. "Klein," Newton said, "was one of the operatives of the United States Department of Justice who probably did more than any other to assist in unraveling the crime of the Labatt kidnapping."[2]

Catharine Klein sent Director Hoover a thank-you card, which read: "Gratefully acknowledging and thanking you for your kind expression of sympathy, Catharine Klein and children."

Southgate, Ky.

My dear Mr. Hoover,

It seems unbelievable that Nelson has been taken from us but it is so.

I have a great task before me with my three children but God is good and I feel sure he will give me strength to carry on.

Words cannot express my appreciation of the kindness you have shown me at this time.

Sincerely yours,

Catharine I. Klein.

8/27/35

◆ Mrs. Klein acknowledges that Nelson is gone and thanks the Director.

Flowers came in to the funeral home from FBI Headquarters in Washington, D.C., and other FBI offices around the country.

Services were held for Agent Klein on the afternoon of August 20, at the A. C. Dobbling & Son Funeral Home in Ft. Thomas, Kentucky. Pallbearers were agents from Klein's office. Many other federal agents and officials attended including United States Attorneys Francis C. Canny and James Cleveland, Assistant U.S. District Marshal George Reeves, and former U.S. Marshal Paul Greswell. [3]

Klein's youngest son, Richard, years later, recalled that his father's brother Eugene lifted him up to the casket, allowing him to kiss his father goodbye. Richard was startled by how cold his father felt.

He was interned at Evergreen Cemetery, Section 57, Lot 37E 1/2, and is the only family member buried at the location, which includes a total of six grave lots. The lots cost a total of $278, which included the grave, lining, and steel vault. The Klein family monument and Klein's headstone purchase was assisted by FBI Agents assigned to the Cincinnati Office.

The day after Klein was buried, Barrett was released from the Fort Hamilton Hospital. The Cincinnati FBI office received the bill for Barrett's care:

Board and Nursing: 5 days @ $6.00	$30.00
Operating Rooms – Casts	$8.00
Medical and Surgical Supplies	$5.00
Laboratory	$5.00
X-ray	$15.00
Gas Gangrene Antitoxin	$4.00
Acacia	$6.00
Total	$73.00

Barrett was taken by ambulance from Fort Hamilton Hospital to Indianapolis City Hospital in Indianapolis, which cost the FBI $10 for the transport. Cincinnati agents Jamie S. Johnson, George F. Bickley, Milton J. Boyd, William E. Robinson, Donald C. McGovern, and Samuel K. McKee made up the security detail. They were taking no chances. Barrett was handed over into the federal custody of a Deputy United States Marshal and examined by a federal doctor the purpose of which was to justify Barrett's hospital stay. The ward's doors and windows were barred, and Barrett was held there in a small, private room. A local police officer was on guard in the ward continuously, and three agents were assigned to the location where they rotated shifts, two of them always on duty. The agents had a room in the hospital for use during their time-off, and they got their meals at the hospital, as well. [4] [5]

INVESTIGATING THE MURDER

The murder investigation of Klein and the automobile thefts by Barrett were investigated jointly under FBI Bureau file number 26-HQ-38858. The Cincinnati office was the office of origin, (file 26-4422[‡]) with the assistance of the Indianapolis FBI office (file 89-2[§]) in whose territory the murder took place.

Just after the shooting, on the same evening, Barrett's automobile and baggage were taken into evidence by Sheriff Clem Slack of Liberty, Indiana. Agents Jamie S. Johnson and Donald McGovern got Barrett's suitcase from the sheriff and inventoried it at the Cincinnati FBI office. It contained the following:

Shoulder holster

Colt New Series .38 W.C.F. Revolver, double action, loaded with four-USC Company .38 W.C.F and 1 REM-UMC .38 W.C.F

1 ladies ring with red stone in case marked, Ideal Jewelers, 602 Vine Street, Cincinnati, OH

1935 Indiana license plate #62-132

Shaving mug and brush

Tooth powder, brush

Clothes brush

Razor

Pocket knife

3 skeleton keys in razor case

2 cakes of soap

Razor strap

Miscellaneous postcards (unused)

Pamphlet (Black Hills Detour)

Notepad containing license and key numbers

Blank stationery and envelope

Grey coat (lightweight)

Fountain pen

1 soiled shirt (laundry mark "JLB")

4 handkerchiefs

3 ties

1 pair of socks

1 glass eye (blue)

1 tube mercurial ointment

1 box aspirin

2 clean shirts

1 knee brace

1 photograph of a girl named Jeanie Arnett Abbott

The G-man and the Diamond King

On August 17, Special Agent Bliss Morton of the Indianapolis FBI office appeared before United States Commissioner Howard B. Young in Indianapolis and filed a complaint charging George W. Barrett with unlawfully killing Special Agent Nelson B. Klein of the Federal Bureau of Investigation, United States Department of Justice, on August 16, 1935 in Union County, Indiana, in violation of 454-A Title 18 U.S.C.

On the same day, Special Agent Howard D. Harris of the Cincinnati FBI office filed a fugitive complaint in Cincinnati for Mabel Barrett and John Laws, who were named as material witnesses. They were committed to the Hamilton County Jail in Cincinnati, John Laws furnishing a $5,000 bond on August 19, while Mabel Barrett was unable to do so and remained in jail.

John Laws was interviewed by SAC Earl J. Connelley of the Cincinnati FBI Office, and again by agents Samuel K. McKee and Howard D. Harris, also of the Cincinnati FBI office. Laws gave them a three-page statement, which is summarized as follows: On the morning of August 16, 1935, after overhearing a conversation between Officers Earl Welch and Ed Riley at the Hamilton Police Department, Laws had a conversation with Officer Welch and learned that George Barrett was being sought by federal officers in connection with an automobile case. Laws then contacted Mabel Barrett and Irwin Brockman and arranged to meet George Barrett. He met with Barrett on the Airport Road near Highway 4 in Hamilton, Ohio, told Barrett that federal officers were looking for him, and that if he went to the Central Motors, in Hamilton, he'd be arrested.[6]

Connelley noted in the FBI file that the Cincinnati office had known for a considerable period of time that Laws had close contact with the Hamilton Police Department. He'd been seen by agents on numerous occasions hanging out at the HPD station. The FBI also knew that Laws had been a police informant for awhile, providing information about stolen automobiles.

Mabel Barrett was interviewed by Special Agent Milton J. Boyd. She said that on August 16 she'd looked out her window and saw John Laws sitting in his car. Laws owned the house she lived in and was there to collect the rent. When she went outside, Laws asked her where her brother-in-law, George Barrett, was; she said she didn't know. She and Laws walked over to Irvin Brockman's house on See Avenue to ask if he knew where George Barrett could be found, but Brockman wasn't home. Mabel said that she and her husband, Gilbert Barrett, had been arrested in Shelbyville, Indiana, for shoplifting and that she had served sixty days in the women's prison at Indianapolis. At the time of her interview, Gilbert was serving a sentence of one to ten years in the Michigan City Prison in Michigan City, Indiana.[7]

LIFE AS A CAR PIRATE

Two days after the shooting, Barrett gave Agents Robert H. Klett and Samuel K. McKee a statement about the various cars he had stolen. It was a long and rambling report, without detail or drama, as though stealing cars was merely another serviceable occupation, such as selling insurance or the collection of bad debt. If, as it has been said, that no harm ever came from reading, then Barrett proved otherwise: in 1930 or 1931, he read several articles about automobile theft rings in and around Richmond and Berea, Kentucky, and he read how they worked. First, the thieves bought a car legitimately, acquiring a bill of sale and title papers. Then they found an identical car, stole it, and changed its identification numbers. The stolen vehicle thus became "legitimate."

Barrett liked the idea and went to work. In June of 1932, he bought a Chevrolet sedan from Central Motors in Hamilton, securing an Ohio bill of sale. He sold it to a dealer in Lexington, Kentucky, and when he spotted an identical car parked on the street in Wilmore, he stole it, drove it to Oklahoma where, using his original bill of sale, sold it to a used car dealer named Homer Horne. Except for the eight-hundred-mile drive, it was easy, and Barrett had a new line of work. Mr. Horne seemed to be the unwitting recipient of a number of cars that came from Ohio.

Barrett bought another Chevrolet from Avondale Auto Sales in Cincinnati, stole its mate off the street in Hamilton, and returned with it to Avondale Auto, who bought it, thinking they were buying back the original car they'd earlier sold to Barrett. He rented a similar coupe in the spring of 1934 from the Hertz Drive-Ur-Self Company in Knoxville, Tennessee, under an assumed name, changed its serial numbers, and drove it to Homer Horne in Oklahoma.

Usually, though, Barrett would buy a car, then steal an identical one, and use the title from the legitimate car for the stolen one. Barrett's cars—with fake serial numbers— turned up all over Kentucky, Indiana, Oklahoma, even California. He once bought a "hot" car from a man in a Hamilton bar for $75, changed its motor numbers, and sold it to a man named Arthur Hock in Hamilton.

Barrett seemed to take pleasure in the circuitous methods of car pirates. He rented a car in St. Louis, for instance, and bought a near-identical one from Central Motors. He secured an Indiana certificate of title in Indianapolis using his new bill of sale and his brother's College Corner address. A short time later, he returned to Indianapolis and secured a duplicate title. Then he took the coupe he'd rented in St. Louis—and

The G-man and the Diamond King

conveniently never returned—changed its serial numbers, and sold it to Arthur Hock for $450. If George Barrett had spent as much time and energy in some legitimate undertaking, he might have been a captain of industry. But Barrett liked the shady side of any street.

He told the agents in his interview that at the time of his arrest, however, that he was driving what he called "a bona fide" car. He actually owned it—legitimate title, no altered serial numbers. He told them he'd learned to file and alter serial numbers by a man in Manchester, Kentucky, whose name may (or may not) have been Blaine Clark. Clark showed him how to file off the motor numbers and how to cut in new numbers with the use of steel dies. After they'd changed the numbers on their first car, Clark told Barrett he'd rent the files and dies to him for $5 for each car in which Barrett used his tools.

Clark, Barrett told the agents, was his own graduate school, the only person who aided him in any way in stealing and transporting cars. Other than Clark—or whoever he was—Barrett was entirely a self-made man.[8]

THE FINAL DETAILS OF GEORGE BARRETT'S HAPHAZARD LIFE

On August 26, McGovern interviewed Edna Parrott, who was living with her brother at College Corner, Ohio. This interview described the real George Barrett and his *modus operandi*. Parrott, who was from Grey Hawk, Kentucky, was 16 at the time of the interview and had met Barrett in September of 1933 while he was selling jewelry in McKee, Kentucky. Two months later, they decided to get married and set a date for June of the following year. Her mother gave permission. In January 1934, they drove to Newport, Kentucky, and—so Parrott thought—got married. She described the witnesses as a Mrs. White and a fellow named Bob but couldn't recall the name of the preacher.[9]

Barrett bought a lot of jewelry in Cincinnati, which he later sold in Mt. Vernon, Kentucky. They next traveled to Knoxville, Tennessee, where Barrett bought nine watches for $60, a diamond ring for $240, and some pistols. They registered at the Central Hotel under the name "George W. Clark and wife."[10]

They next traveled to Booneville, Kentucky, where Barrett again sold some jewelry. They went on to Hazard, where they stayed at the Grand Hotel under the name of "J.D. Long and wife." This is where Barrett was arrested by the police for adultery. Barrett never discussed his business with her nor why he registered under fictitious names. When arrested, he had $831 in cash, five diamond rings, nineteen pistols, and twenty-three watches. Barrett sent his brother John to claim the items, but the police wouldn't release them. Barrett was fined $50 for adultery and for selling an illegal gun. The next day the police told Parrott that her marriage license was a fake. She left Barrett and went back to live with her parents in Grey Hawk.[11]

Parrott later saw Barrett three times, once in December of 1934 for a few minutes and again for a short time in January of 1935 and the spring of 1935, at her sister's residence in Grey Hawk. In a touch of fate, she moved to College Corner to live with her brother, Robert Parrott, the day before Barrett was involved in the shooting. She did not visit the shooting location.

In early September of 1935, United States Attorney Valentine Nolan in Indianapolis decided it was no longer necessary to keep Mabel Barrett in custody. She had been unable to make bail due to lack of funds, and Nolan also doubted that he would use her as a witness at Barrett's trial.

On September 17, the FBI laboratory provided its report back to Cincinnati, Indianapolis, and the FBI headquarters in Washington, after having conducted tests on the following: Bisley model .45 caliber Colt revolver, serial number 318989; two fatal bullets extracted from the body of Agent Klein; Colt new series .38 WCF revolver, serial number 328935 (taken from Barrett); and five unexploded cartridges from the Colt new series .38 WCF revolver.

Nelson Klein's Bureau identification card and its final disposition.

The G-man and the Diamond King

Examiner F. B. Harrington wrote, "the two fatal bullets extracted from the body of Agent Klein have been compared microscopically with test bullets fired from the Bisley model .45 caliber Colt revolver, serial number 318989. The condition of the evidence bullets due to impact are such that the marks are relatively few and rather poor, but sufficient similarities in the markings exist to indicate that the fatal bullets were probably fired from revolver number 318989. Because there are only a few remaining marks, an identification would be difficult to substantiate photographically. Two of the unexploded .38 WCF cartridges were used for test purposes. The other evidence consisting of the two revolvers, fatal bullets, and three unexploded cartridges are being returned under separate cover. It is desired that the two revolvers be forwarded to the laboratory when they have served their purpose as evidence." [12]

On October 9, Irvin Brockman of See Avenue in Hamilton was interviewed by Special Agents Robert H. Klett and J.S. Johnson of the Cincinnati office. Brockman, who'd been arrested a number of times for liquor violations, assault, and disturbing the peace, said he'd known George Barrett for twenty years, in both Ohio and Kentucky. On August 16, Brockman had gone to Law's pool room, and Laws told him he needed to talk to Barrett, either in person or by telephone. When Brockman returned home, he saw Barrett near his house, sitting in his car.

The two of them went to the Green Lantern on Dixie Highway, where Barrett telephoned Laws to arrange a meeting. Brockman went to pick up Laws and brought him to where Barrett wanted to meet—White City Park. Brockman stayed in the car while Laws and Barrett went off to talk. Barrett then had Laws go by bus to the Hamilton Hotel to pick up Barrett's belongings and pay his bill. [13]

When he returned, Laws and Barrett drove to College Corner in Barrett's vehicle, headed for the house of his brother, John. It was then about 3 p.m. On the way, Barrett stopped and changed the license plates on the vehicle. "I'm going to change plates because federal men are looking for me," Barrett told Brockman. "That was what John Laws wanted with me: to tell me the federal men were after me."

"I don't want to be with you, George," Brockman said.

"You don't have to worry," Barrett said, "they ain't got nothing on me."

Barrett parked a block and a half away from his brother's house, and as they parked, Brockman saw a black sedan with two men in it. Brockman told Barrett it was the law, but Barrett, intent on reaching his brother's house, said nothing. McGovern saw the man he thought was Barrett, followed him, and saw him go into John Barrett's yard. Klein remained with the car and McGovern quickly returned; they were sure they had their man, but wary of Barrett and his reputation, they waited for help from the Union County

Sheriff's Office. Unknown to the agents, Barrett was intent of reaching his brother's house because his Colt .45 was there.

Brockman, nervous, remained in John Barrett's house only a few minutes before he left, being given a ride back to Hamilton with John Barrett's son, Hardin. George Barrett said to Brockman that he was headed west.[14]

The FBI conducted hundreds of interviews in the murder/car theft investigation. It reached to all sections of the United States with FBI offices in Atlanta (file 26-230), Boston (file 26-142), Detroit (file 26-5172), Cleveland (file 26-112), El Paso (file # unknown), Los Angeles (file 26-3618), Louisville (file 89-3), Nashville (file 26-463), Oklahoma City (file 26-4868), Philadelphia (file 89-3), Phoenix (file 26-40), St. Louis (file 26-4640), San Antonio (file 26-5561) and San Francisco (file 26-2534) assisting.

Through interviews with Barrett, communication with the Automobile Protective & Information Bureau, and the FBI files, the Bureau determined that Barrett was responsible for the theft of at least twenty-six automobiles. They ranged in year of manufacture from 1931 to 1935 and included one Plymouth Deluxe coupe, one Desoto coupe, and twenty-four Chevrolet coaches, coupes, or sedans.

But George Barrett had now graduated from auto theft. And while he had killed before, he hadn't killed an agent of the Federal Bureau of Investigation. He was now in the big leagues, and it was unlikely he could buy his way out this time, even if he was "the diamond king."

ENDNOTES

* The FBI has the following funds which allocate monies to the families of agents killed in the line of duty:

The Special Agents Insurance Fund (SAIF) is an FBI-sponsored insurance program that pays for the death of a Special Agent, whether job-related or not, and even pays in the event of a suicide death that occurs more than two years after the agent joined the SAIF. The fund was established to make sure that the beneficiaries of a Special Agent who dies while employed by the Bureau would have immediate funds to take care of their needs while awaiting other benefit payments. The SAIF pays $30,000 within one workday of notification to FBIHQ of the death of the Special Agent.

The G-man and the Diamond King

The cost to Special Agents is an initial $20.00 fee and then periodic $20.00 assessments.

The Charles S. Ross Fund was established as a memorial to a Special Agent killed in the line of duty and every Special Agent automatically belongs to the Fund. The Ross Fund pays only when a Special Agent loses his/her life in the line of duty. The amount payable by the Ross Fund is periodically adjusted to reflect increases in the cost of living. The current payment amount is $15,750, payable within one workday after FBIHQ notification. Membership in the Charles S. Ross Fund is free to all Special Agents.

The Public Safety Officers' Benefit (PSOB) covers all federal, state, and local law enforcement officers, firefighters, rescue workers, and any other "public safety officer" who loses his/her life in the line of duty. The PSOB pays only if an agent is killed in the line of duty and is survived by a current spouse, child, or parent. The amount of the benefit is adjusted each year for changes in the Consumer Price Index. The current PSOB benefit is $283,385. All FBI Special Agents are automatically covered by this program, premium-free. (*www.fbijobs.gov/3321.asp*)

[†] W.R. Glavin was born in Mahanoy City, Pennsylvania, and grew up in Pittsburgh, where he worked for the Postal Telegraph Company. He joined the Marine Corps after moving to Washington, D.C., in the mid 1920s, and for five years taught business at the Marine Corps Institute. Following his discharge he attended Southeastern University in Washington, where he received a B.C.S. degree. On April 6, 1931, Glavin entered on duty with the FBI as a Special Agent. He was appointed head of the Chief Clerk's Office in 1936 and later was promoted to inspector. Glavin was one of the agents present when on May 1, 1936, Hoover lead the arrest of Alvin Francis "Creepy Karpis" Karpowicz in New Orleans. Glavin died on June 19, 1986. (*The FBI: A Comprehensive Reference Guide*)

[‡] Under the current FBI Investigative Classification system, "26" matters are Interstate Transportation of Stolen Motor Vehicles (ITSMV).

[§] "89B" is designated for assaulting or killing a federal officer.

KENTUCKY HILLS

"No one can arrest me," was the oft-repeated boast of the triple murderer, George Barrett (*right*), who, for twenty-two years, evaded punishment for his crimes. But Justice caught up with him when astute G-men entered the case

In Manchester, Kentucky (*above*), George Barrett showed his characteristic cowardice when he fled for shelter while the man he had been hired to protect was slain

By

RICHARD HIRSCH

Barrett rides into the courtroom in a wheelchair, legs extended.

The U.S. vs. George Barrett

7

THE INDICTMENT

The federal indictment of Barrett for the murder of FBI Agent Nelson Klein was filed on August 30, 1935, in Indianapolis. On November 5, Barrett, gray haired, looking very middle-aged and incapacitated—one of the newspapers referred to him as "the Kentucky desperado who doesn't look the part"—appeared in federal court in Indianapolis. He sat in a wheelchair with both legs in splints. His legs were laid straight out and rested on a board attached to his chair. There was no indication of pain in his expression or any indication that he had killed Klein. Barrett was going to be the second person to be tried for murder under a new federal statute providing trial in federal courts for killing a government agent. If convicted, and the jury failed to recommend mercy, Barrett would be hanged. Either way, he was about to make history.[1]

Barrett was assisted to federal court from the Indianapolis City Hospital because both of his legs had been shattered by bullets during the shootout with Klein and McGovern. Eight FBI Agents who had worked with Klein were led by SAC Harold H. Reinecke[†] of the Indianapolis FBI office, standing guard over Barrett as a deputy United States marshal pushed his wheelchair into the courtroom.[3]

Barrett first pled guilty to two charges of violating the National Motor Vehicle Theft Act, then Val Nolan, United States attorney, read a statement charging Barrett with murder.

"How do you plead?" Judge Robert C. Baltzell asked.

"Your honor, not guilty," Barrett said, then adjusted his glasses.

Previously, the judge had overruled a demur filed by Everett E. Rice, a Hamilton, Ohio, defense attorney who challenged the court's jurisdiction in the case. Rice asked that the trial be held in Liberty, Indiana, Union County, where the slaying took place, but the judge said there were no facilities in Liberty for a federal trial and that he had authority to designate the place.

The judge set the trial date for December 2, 1935; Barrett remained still and expressionless. He was then pushed through the corridor to the elevator and into a waiting automobile for his return to city hospital. Barrett with his leg in a cast would still be chained to his bed and guarded by FBI Agents night and day.[4]

The new statute

"The first-degree murder charge that Barrett faced was applied under what was then a new but well-known statute that made the murder of a government agent a federal offense.* The statute, enacted in 1934, was brought about by the murder of a number of agents in the 1920s and early 1930s. At the time of these murders, there was no federal law in place addressing these crimes, and as a result, they were heard in state courts. This led to a disparity in sentences; in one instance, the killers served less than thirty-five years. The new law sought to remedy this situation by mandating the death penalty in first-degree murders of federal agents unless—and only unless—the jury qualified its verdict by specifying that capital punishment was not to be applied." [2]

Director Hoover, along with Courtney Ryley Cooper, wrote an article titled "The Meanest Man I Ever Knew" for the April 1937 edition of *The American Magazine*. It's highly doubtful that Director Hoover ever met Barrett. Hoover suggested that Barrett had no intention of ever pleading guilty to the murder of Agent Klein and that he was like every other criminal who believed that if he got out of one scrape he could get out of another. He believed that Barrett thought he would get out of the arrest with ease. He would plead self-defense, saying the agents were gangsters. He would also pretend to be crippled and throw himself at the mercy of the jury.

On the morning of October 11, Dr. Robert Dwyer, the new government doctor at Indianapolis, examined Barrett, still confined in the prison ward at the city hospital. The bandages and cast were removed from his left leg. The leg was bent at the knee and Barrett was instructed to frequently massage the leg. The cast and bandages were replaced and Barrett said he had no pain in his left leg. The bandages from the right leg were also removed, and it was found to be in more serious condition but improving. The cast and bandages were then replaced on the right leg. The doctor suggested to the agents guarding Barrett that there was no reason why he couldn't be walking with the aid of a cane in two weeks.[5]

On October 19, Dr. Dwyer again visited Barrett at the city hospital. The cast and bandages on his right leg were removed. Barrett was then told he would be immediately taken in a wheelchair to the lavatory to have his legs soaked in hot water to stimulate circulation, and that this procedure should be done often. Barrett was able to bend his right leg to some extent, but when he reached a certain point a feeling of stiffness and pain overcame him.[6]

Crutches were obtained so that Barrett could start putting some of his weight on them. The doctor wanted him to learn to walk again, starting with small steps. Barrett laid aside his Bible that he had been reading. His one eye got this wild look in it, and he stated, "I can't do it!"

Barrett came up with a number of excuses, and the surgeon brushed them off. After Barrett had run out of excuses, he was lifted up from his bed by the prison guards onto the crutches. Barrett winced and tears came running down his face.

"Pain is killing me terrible," he said, "like knives runnin' through my flesh whenever I touch my feet to the floor!"

"You haven't touched them to the floor," the surgeon told him.

Barrett continued whining; the surgeon smiled, turned to the agents and said, "He's getting his sympathy plea ready, blaming the G-men that he was crippled."

He told Barrett that if he didn't use his legs at some point, he would never be able to use them. During the day, Barrett never moved his legs freely, but at night while asleep he was observed by the guards moving them as though they had never been injured.[7]

THE TRIAL

Monday, December 2, 1935

The case of United States versus George W. Barrett began in Federal court with the Honorable Robert C. Baltzell, Judge of the District Court of the United States for the Southern District of Indiana, Indianapolis Division presiding.

The government's case was presented by United States Attorney Valentine Francis Nolan. Nolan was the son of John J. Nolan, the mayor of Evansville, Indiana, who was married to Jeannette Covert, an author of children's book who was the daughter of a former Evansville postmaster. Nolan was a war veteran who previously served as the Evansville city attorney.

Assistant United States attorneys Howard Caughran and Paul Pfister assisted in the prosecution. Barrett, meanwhile, was represented by attorneys Everett Rice and Edward Ellis of Hamilton. The prosecution of the case was based on the indictment returned by the federal grand jury of the southern district of Indiana on August 30, which indicted Barrett for first degree murder.

◆ Judge Robert Baltzell, a man not without empathy, tries the Barrett case.

◆ Val Nolan, the prosecuting attorney, was intent on getting a guilty verdict, without mercy.

The courtroom was not without a certain amount of tension. Even before the trial got underway, a nervous onlooker saw that defense attorney Rice had a large bulge in his back pocket, and the United States marshal was notified. When the marshal frisked Rice, he saw that Rice was merely carrying some rolled-up legal papers.

Two doctors testified before Judge Baltzell that Barrett was physically able to withstand the rigors of a trial,[8] and this was followed by jury selection, which took less than an hour and a half, as they were all willing to consider the death penalty. It consisted of nine farmers, two automobile dealers, and a sawmill operator—all men. Judge Baltzell arranged for the jurors—under the watch of two deputy U.S. marshals—to be housed at the nearby Claypool Hotel when court was not in session. Members of the jury were the following:

The G-man and the Diamond King

Floyd Custinger	Age 60, from Franklin/ Johnson County farmer	Married with one son, a Democrat and a member of the Christian church
Russell Rothrock	Age 36 to 40, from White Cloud/Harrison county sawmill operator	Married with three or four children, a Republican and a member of the United Brethren church
Ray G. Hornaday	Age 45 to 55, from Montgomery/Daviess County farmer	Married with two sons, a Republican and a member of the Methodist church
Ward Borter	Age 35, from Newberry/ Greene County farmer	Married with two sons, a Democrat and a member of the Methodist church
J.D. Bolander	Age 53, a Connersville/ Fayette county automobile dealer	Married with two children, a Republican and a member of the Christian Science church
Fred Secrest (Foreman)	Age 55 to 60, from Martinsville/Morgan County farmer	Married with one son and one daughter, a Democrat and member of Christian church
Harold E. Selig	Age 45 to 50, from Corydon/Harrison County farmer	Married with three or four children, a Republican and member of the Baptist Church
Fielding M. Colbert	Age 63, from Washington/Daviess County farmer	Married, a Republican and member of the Methodist church
James I. Clem	Age 55 to 60, Mooresville/Morgan County farmer	Married with two sons and one daughter, a Democrat and member of the Christian church
Clevy O. Drake	Age 45, from Farmersburg/Sullivan County farmer	Married with four boys and one girl, a Democrat and member of the Baptist church
Joseph Starkey	Age 66, from Kingman/ Fountain County automobile dealer	Married with three boys and three girls, a Republican and member of the United Brethren church
John Bunnell	Age 58, from Hagerstown/Wayne County farmer	Married with two children, a Democrat and member of the Baptist church

The federal courthouse in Indianapolis, as it appeared in 1935.

◆ The courtroom where Barrett was tried has remained virtually unchanged since his trial.

The G-man and the Diamond King

The Judge administered the oath and told them that they could not read any newspapers containing articles of the case, talk to any family or friends about what was going on in the courtroom, or discuss their feelings or thoughts with any of the other jurors until all the evidence and testimony had been presented to them. Once this was done, they would begin deliberations.

In late October, SAC E. J. Connelly of the Cincinnati FBI office, at the behest of United States Attorney Val Nolan, discussed with Catharine Klein the possibility of her testifying at the trial and the children being present. Mrs. Klein thought it would be an ordeal, and she would like for all of them to be spared but if Nolan felt their presence was essential then, of course, she and the children would be there. Thus Mrs. Klein was in the courtroom with her three children: sons Nelson "Bud" Jr., age 9; Richard, age 7, and daughter Barbara Ann age 3, blonde, wearing a yellow dress, and sitting on her mother's lap.

"Judge Baltzell ordered the separation of witnesses, and she was the first witness for the government." She was described by the media as young, pretty, and slender with reddish hair, wearing a black tailored dress with touches of white. She testified that she "saw her husband alive for the last time on the morning of August 16, when he told her goodbye." She also testified on his death, funeral services, and burial.[9]

◆ The jurors were ensconced in the Claypool Hotel, ruined by fire in 1967.

District Court of the United States of America
Southern District of Indiana
Indianapolis Division

THE PRESIDENT OF THE UNITED STATES OF AMERICA

To __Catherine I. Klein, Southgate, Kentucky, (widow of Nelson B. Klein)__
__(if unable to locate, contact Fed. Bur. Inv.__
__Office, Cincinnati, Ohio)__

YOU ARE HEREBY COMMANDED that laying aside all and singular your business and excuses, you be and appear in the District Court of the United States for the __Southern District of Indiana__ at the Courthouse, in the city of __Indianapolis__, in said district, on the __2nd__ day of __December__ A. D. 19__35__, at __9:30__ o'clock __A__ M. of said day, then and there to testify and give evidence on behalf of the United States, and not to depart the Court without leave thereof, or of the District Attorney.

Hereof fail not, under penalty of whatever may befall you thereon.

WITNESS, the Honorable __Robert C. Baltzell__

_____ Judge

(Seal)

of said District Court of the United States, this __2nd__ day of __November__, A. D. 19__35__, and in the __160th__ year of the Independence of the United States of America.

__Albert C. Sogemeier__
Clerk.

By __Mary Lou Hostettler__
7—1472   _Deputy Clerk._

The summons for Catharine Klein to appear in court for the Barrett trial.

A reluctant Mrs. Klein and her three small children, as photographed at the trial.

Dr. William L. Porter, the coroner of Union County, Indiana, testified that Klein had died of "gunshot wounds and shock," [10] and Dr. Douglas B. Remsen, the pathologist at Christ Hospital in Cincinnati, described the five bullet locations in Klein's body. [11]

On the first day of the trial, Agent Donald McGovern testified about Barrett's method of operation of stolen cars, and of finding him in College Corner, Indiana. McGovern was cross-examined by Barrett's attorney, Rice, who asked about their first sighting of Barrett, "Why didn't you arrest him?"

The G-man and the Diamond King

McGovern said they knew Barrett was dangerous and that he'd shot his own mother, and they wished to avoid the chance of a shooting on one of the town's busy streets. [12]

Agent McGovern was only one of several G-men who testified, giving their testimony "as coldly and impersonal as a steel trap," wrote one of the newspapers covering the trial.

Tuesday, December 3, 1935

On Tuesday, Agent McGovern identified his partner's bloodstained brown suit with bullet holes, which was introduced as evidence, along with photographs of the scene. Edward Ellis, Barrett's other attorney, jumped to his feet and objected to the introduction of this evidence, suggesting that it was too gruesome for the jury to see. The United States attorney Nolan and Ellis engaged in a heated argument, and the judge overruled the objection.

McGovern went on to describe Barrett, who was wearing a short-sleeved shirt and carrying a package covered with a face towel. When the two agents drove near, Barrett turned from his own car and ran down an alley, with Klein running after him. McGovern ran around an alleyway garage to cut Barrett off, then he heard shots.

Once around the garage, he saw his partner on the ground and Barrett, holding a revolver, ducking behind a tree. McGovern fired at Barrett's exposed leg, and Barrett fell. Although McGovern didn't know this at the time, Klein was mortally wounded.

McGovern was asked to identify both Klein's and Barrett's weapons. Prosecuting attorney Nolan also asked McGovern to show the court how a single-action revolver can be shot rapidly by trick manipulation, or what is known as "fanning," done by holding the trigger with one hand and using the other to "fan" the hammer quickly, creating a rapid firing.[13]

McGovern's demonstration was not fully appreciated by the judge, who cautioned the agent by saying, "Don't point that gun in *this* direction."

Ora Brown, the postmaster of College Corner, testified that he took photographs of Agent Klein at the scene of the shooting, which were introduced into evidence. Rice objected to introduction of the photographs because of their graphic nature, and his objection was overruled by the judge.[16]

Charles B. Walke, a deputy sheriff from Hamilton, testified he was contacted by Agent Klein to assist in the arrest of Barrett. He arrived only in time to help get Barrett into an ambulance.

"You wouldn't shoot a man like this, would you sheriff?" Barrett said to Walke.

"It would depend on the circumstances," Walke answered. "Why did you shoot that man?"

"Us Kentuckians carry guns and we carry 'em to shoot," Barrett said.

Walker said that at no time during his conversation with Barrett did Barrett ever suggest that he had acted in self-defense.[17]

Fanning

The technique of "fanning" actually does increase the rate of fire, but it's mostly used in novelty shooting demonstrations. The idea of it seems to have been largely created by western movies in which gunmen "fan" their weapons in gunfights. There's a famous fanning sequence in *Butch and the Sundance Kid* when Butch and the Kid fight Bolivian bandits, and Val Kilmer's Doc Holliday "fans" during the fight at the O.K. Corral in the movie *Tombstone* (something it's doubtful the real Doc, who had a reputation as deadly with a gun, would have done). Fanning even became gender neutral when Sharon Stone did it in *The Quick and the Dead*.

Most experts, though, find the technique, let us say, *fanciful*. None other than the famed lawman Wyatt Earp said, "In all my life as a frontier peace officer, I did not know of a really proficient gunfighter who had anything but contempt for the gun-fanner, or the man who literally shot from the hip."

And there was also a classic example from an 1879 gunfight in Dodge City. There, Cockeyed Frank Loving and a buffalo hunter named Levi Richardson faced off in Dodge City. They both drew, Richardson "fanned" five shots—and missed. Loving (in spite of his nickname) patiently waited, aimed carefully, fired once, and killed Richardson dead. [14] [15]

Howard Harris[‡], who had been assigned to the Cincinnati FBI office for five years, was Acting Special Agent-In-Charge (SAC) in the absence of E.J. Connelley, and he testified that he sent Klein and McGovern to arrest Barrett, without a warrant. He said no warrant was needed if a federal violation was determined.

Barrett's attorney, Rice, tried to show that the agents were only seeking to question Barrett, and they had no authority to fire on him. Harris said the FBI had established motor vehicle theft through the Bureau's teletype system.[§] Rice wanted to see the document and the judge told him to get with the prosecutor at the break.[18]

The G-man and the Diamond King

Connelley[11], the Cincinnati SAC since 1932, was the first witness to testify on December 4. He had been out of the Cincinnati division on the day of the shooting, handling the Weyerhauser kidnapping case in Washington state. He directed the search for the kidnapped boy, who was returned unarmed; the culprits were caught. Director Hoover personally ordered Connelley to fly back to Cincinnati on the night of the killing. Connelley said he had never met Barrett until that evening at the Fort Hamilton Hospital when he interviewed him. Doctors said Barrett had been given small doses of morphine for pain but that it would be okay to talk with him. Connelley considered Klein not only a co-worker but also a close personal friend.[19]

Samuel K. McKee#, a Special Agent assigned to the Cincinnati FBI office, testified that he had guarded Barrett at the hospital, and Barrett made a number of incriminating statements to him. He also said Barrett asked him to help him kill himself. "He remarked that he had just as soon be dead…he said he had nothing else to live for, that he wanted to meet his dear old mother in heaven and explain to

Agent Klein's family appears dazed by the events around them.

her why he had killed her, and he said, 'Would you help me over to the window?' and I said, 'Yes, I would,' and I said, 'I will push the screen up for you, but I don't think you would jump, I don't think you have got nerve enough.' That was the end of the conversation." [20][21]

Irvin Brockman of See Avenue in Hamilton, a 33-year-old former Kentuckian and a distant cousin of Barrett, spent approximately two hours on the stand. Brockman found himself in a bind: he testified that he was a friend, yet he had also given a statement to the FBI on October 9 implicating Barrett. It was Brockman who had driven with Barrett to College Corner on August 16, the day of the shooting.

Brockman then hid out until October 9, when he voluntarily went to the Cincinnati FBI office to explain what he knew of the shooting. Brockman was a reluctant witness, and he didn't look at Barrett while he testified. Sometimes he didn't answer the question, or he gave one-word answers. The prosecution was quick to catch Brockman in contradictory statements about whether Barrett believed he was being pursued by feuding Kentuckians or federal agents.[22]

Agatha M. McDonough, a 39 year old College Corner resident, in whose backyard the shooting occurred, said she was saying goodbye to company on her front porch when she heard a noise that sounded like the backfire from a car. Then she saw a man—it would prove to be Agent McGovern—run down the street with a gun in his hand. She realized that what she heard were gunshots fired in her backyard. She ran into the house, heard more gunfire, and was confused about where to go. One bullet crashed through the kitchen window. When the shots stopped, she opened the backdoor, and saw Barrett lying near a tree. "I shot him," he said to her, "but he shot me first. I think he is a government man." [23]

She went over to him and asked him if he was hurt. He appeared very pale, and she thought he was going to die. Barrett said he was shot in the legs and kept waving his revolver around. Barrett said the weapon was empty, and he even disengaged the barrel to show her, which didn't help because she knew nothing about guns. It was at this time that she saw Agent Klein's body, and she thought that at any moment he might rise and begin shooting again. She then took the gun out of Barrett's hand, and later she gave it to the Butler County sheriff, John Schumacher. [24]

Lathonia Forbes of North Main Street in Oxford followed Mrs. McDonough into the yard and said to Barrett, "Who is that over there?"

"A government man; I shot him," Barrett answered.

"Why was that?" Mrs. Forbes asked.

"I was in a little trouble, and he was after me." [25]

Paul "Felix" McDonough, husband of Agatha McDonough, was two blocks from his home and heard the shooting, whereupon he drove straight home and saw in his yard his wife, Mrs. Forbes, George Barrett, and the dead body of Agent Klein. McDonough had a conversation with Barrett about five minutes after the shooting, and he asked him who the dead man was.

"He is a government man," Barrett answered, "and it was either him or me and I beat him to the draw. They think I have got a hot car, but I haven't." [26]

John Laws, the 39-year-old Hamilton man and operator of a Grand Boulevard café, testified that he learned at the Hamilton police headquarters that the federal men wanted Barrett. He went to find Barrett, who asked, "Who wants me? Does the police want me?"

"No," Laws answered, "but I think the federal men do."

"What do they want with me?"

"Maybe they want to talk to you about automobiles."

Shortly afterward, Barrett drove to College Corner. [27]

The G-man and the Diamond King

On the afternoon of December 4, attorney Nolan read the statement George Barrett had given to agents on August 18 when he was still in Fort Hamilton Hospital. He told about living in Hamilton for the past year, under the name of James L. Black, and using the town as his headquarters while he came and went to other places, always in connection with stealing automobiles. A week before the shootout with Klein and McGovern, he was using his brother John and his family in College Corner to pick up his mail, which he was having sent to the post office there under his own name and the name "George Ball."

He told of his meeting with John Laws, who warned him that federal agents had set traps around town for him. Laws had been at the Hamilton police department and heard officers talk about Barrett and stolen cars, and they knew Barrett's physical description, down to his glass eye.

He had another acquaintance, Irvin Brockman, pay his hotel bill and clear out his things, as he was planning on driving to San Antonio, Texas. First, however, he would visit his brother in College Corner, where he had a Colt .45 revolver. At his brother's house, he got the gun, wrapped in either an old cloth or a newspaper, from a dresser drawer and, leaving it covered, he walked back to his car with it in his hand. He remembered loading it about two weeks before when he returned from a trip to St. Louis, but he wasn't sure whether it was loaded with five or six bullets.

The statement continued:

I walked back to my car with a gun in my hand. As I approach my car I noticed a big car driving up. This car stopped and I noticed two men in it started to get out of the car. Either one or both these men said something to me, but I cannot recall exactly what they said. However, from what they said I knew they were either federal officers to arrest me or someone who had come to take me for a ride. At the time I was thinking both of what John Laws had told me and of the fact that I had heard that some enemies from Manchester, Kentucky, were planning to take me for a ride.

There was an alley near where my car was parked and I started down this alley with the intention of getting away if it was possible. A short distance down the alley I turned to the left and ran for cover to a tree located about 15 or 20 yards from the alley. One of the men followed me down the alley. As I was running toward the tree I unwrapped my gun and had it in my right hand.

I do not know whether I fired first or whether the man who followed me down the alley fired first but we both began firing at each other. I was hit in my left knee and took cover behind the tree. At about this time I saw the second man about 25 yards to my right and he had a gun in his hand. I fired one shot at him and he fired at me. At about this time I was hit in the right knee and I fell to the ground. I saw the second man run out of my sight and again turned toward the first man. I fired at him again and saw him fall to the ground.

I fired until my gun was empty and until it was taken from my hand by some woman. This woman asked me if the gun was empty and put it in the halfcocked notch and turned the cylinder to the left and saw that three or four chambers had been exploded. I became nauseated at this time and I remembered taking my gun and handing it to the woman. The man whom I did not know also came up almost immediately. I talked about the woman and the man, but cannot remember what I said to them. I believe, however that anything I said to them was the truth is I had no reason for lying. A crowd gathered in a few minutes. Short time later Sheriff Schumacher from Hamilton arrived and I was taken to the Fort Hamilton Hospital. The Sheriff from Indiana arrived sometime after Sheriff Schumacher, but I was not taken to the hospital until his arrival.

I have read this statement which consists of four pages, and know the contents to be the truth and to be composed of substance furnished by me to Agent McKee.

George W. Barrett

Barrett's statement was made in the presence of Cincinnati SAC Connelley and witnessed by Agents Samuel K. McKee and Robert H. Klett. [28]

Thursday, December 5, 1935

John Barrett, George Barrett's brother, testified on Thursday that his brother was "a pretty good shot, better than me." John told about a four-hour gun battle that George had been in in Kentucky, which was intended to support the defense plea that George Barrett feared reprisal by feuding Kentuckians, and that he mistook Klein for a down-home enemy when he fired. John said he, George, and two other men went to Manchester, Kentucky, in September of 1932, and a typical Kentucky gang war started in the street outside the Potter Hotel.

He said he lay on the floor for four hours, hearing the bullets rip through the Potter Hotel, and when it was all over he went outside and the other two men were dead on the ground. This, John said, was the experience that led George to believe the members of the Kentucky gang who killed his two friends were after him as well. [29]

George Barrett's own testimony, including cross-examination, lasted for five hours, jumping from one subject to another until he finally discussed the killing of Agent Klein.

Barrett used the "Battle of Manchester" to explain his constant fear of Kentucky gangsters: In that September 1932 incident, Barrett, John Brockman (the brother of Irvin Brockman), and Barrett's brothers, John and Gilbert, were walking from their hotel to the courthouse with Frank Baker, the Commonwealth attorney of the 27th Judicial District of Kentucky, when, suddenly, three men began firing with rifles from the courthouse windows.

The G-man and the Diamond King

The firing, supplemented by other guns on a hill some two hundred and fifty yards away, went on for hours. When it stopped, John Brockman and Frank Baker were dead.

Barrett said that in the spring of 1934, he was in Gray Hawk and Tyner, Kentucky—little Jackson County villages—to deliver a ladies wristwatch he had sold when he saw a large car occupied by two of the men he'd seen on the morning of the Manchester gun battle. The two men brought their rifles to their shoulders, whereupon Barrett, who was in his automobile, drove quickly away, followed by the occupants of the other automobile, whom he managed to evade.

He said that he went back to McKee, Kentucky, a few times after the killing of Baker and Brockman, but for his safety he did so only when there were lots of people in town. When he heard about the Manchester assassination of one Bobby Baker—a cousin of the assassinated Frank Baker—in June of 1935, he drove from Hamilton where he'd been living and, out of concerns for his safety, went to El Paso, Texas, then crossed the border into Mexico.[30]

Barrett explained that he dyed his hair black and bought blue glasses in an effort to hide from those who were looking for him. Attorney Nolan said in the courtroom that Barrett had dyed his hair on the same day (August 1935) that two detectives from the Covington Police Department were looking for him, wanting to discuss Barrett's purchase of too many automobile keys from a Covington locksmith.

"I had been expecting the federal officers to arrest me at any time during the last year on account of my hot car deals," Barrett said. With that statement, made late in the afternoon of December 6, Barrett destroyed his own defense for killing Agent Klein, which had been that he feared outlaws in a Kentucky blood feud were out to get him. Barrett had trapped himself with his own intemperate words.[31]

Friday, December 6, 1935

When court opened on Friday morning, defense attorney Rice caused a stir when he had the jury removed from the courtroom and complained to the judge that the G-Men were intimidating his witnesses. LeRoy Roark, a restaurant owner from Hamilton, had been fingerprinted and questioned by FBI agents. Rice said that what happened to Roark had gotten around and all the defense witnesses were scared. The FBI provided a statement that Roark was questioned for fifteen minutes and was not arrested.

Sylvester Little, a Kentucky Commonwealth attorney, testified about feudist shootings. Attorney Rice asked him, "Is it necessary to carry guns in Kentucky?" The prosecution objected, and the judge sustained the objection. "Kentucky is still in the United States, you know," he said.

Then Rice asked Little if Barrett would be killed if he went back to Manchester.

"Yes, I think so," Little said. [32]

Elizabeth Ecker of Park Avenue in Hamilton—described by the media as a handsome woman of 69—testified that Barrett had roomed at her home for a year, leaving the night of August 15, 1935. She said that "everybody who came to the house liked him" and that the neighborhood children were crazy about him. To her, he was known as James L. Black, and her 13-year-old granddaughter, Leah, called him "Uncle Jim." Barrett had spoken of selling cars, jewels, diamonds, and watches, but never discussed stealing cars. [33]

Other Testimony

College Corner residents Helen Bone and Otis Miller both testified seeing George Barrett carrying a package wrapped in a white cloth. Louis Zimmerman, the night clerk at the Hamilton Hotel, identified a photograph of Barrett as registered in the name of James L. Black, and he provided registration records showing Barrett registered as Black on August 10. Spencer Maxwell, the hotel's day clerk, testified that a man named Brockman came to the hotel with a note from Black, paid his bill, and requested Black's baggage. [34] And Milton Tritsch, the Covington, Kentucky, locksmith, testified that Barrett bought so many keys to Chevrolet automobiles that he became suspicious and notified the Covington police department. A humorous moment took place when Attorney Nolan asked Tritsch his occupation and Tritsch replied, "I operate the most modern locksmith shop in northern Kentucky." [35]

Saturday, December 7, 1935

The closing arguments were, as court historian Doria Lynch would say later, "passionate and dramatic." U.S. attorney Nolan paced about the courtroom and said, "I say to you, George Barrett, that there are many crimes within your breast that have gone unpunished. If you had a thousand lives you could not atone for them all. You will get justice in this court, nothing more, nothing less. You are not being prosecuted by a Kentucky cousin who so obviously protects you that he is reprimanded by the court. You are not being judged by a jury of Kentucky's hillers, but you will get justice." [36]

Then he addressed the jurors. "If you invoke the law of self-defense in this case, you will turn this nation into a shambles. Every Barrett in the country will take such a verdict as a right to shoot down Federal officers. We might as well close this courtroom and turn it into a morgue for dead Special Agents." [37]

The G-man and the Diamond King

And then his conclusion: "I ask in the name of Mrs. Klein and those three babies, and in the name of every decent man and woman in the country, that you do your duty. I ask you, gentlemen, to face this case with the same courage that Nelson Klein faced this outlaw. I ask you to omit those words, 'without capital punishment.' Don't weaken. Don't be lily-livered in this case."

Mrs. Klein, meanwhile, wept softly.

There was a short recess, then the defense attorney, Rice, began his closing arguments. He made frequent biblical references in trying to save Barrett, and he characterized the G-Men as "schoolboy detectives." Then he tried flattery, complimenting Judge Baltzell on his deportment and indicating the southern district of Indiana was lucky to have "a man of his type, a man who could smile like Will Rogers." ** The judge, however, wasn't buying the flattery and told Rice to get on with his closing argument. [38]

"I have suffered the most of anyone in this trial," Rice said to the jury, "because I've had the greatest burden." It was a crafty attempt, but it was doubtful anyone believed Rice, particularly not Barrett, who spent most of the trial in his wheelchair, sitting and staring solemnly at his useless feet, still clad in hospital slippers. "And what was that burden?" Rice went on. "It was fighting all the facilities and forces of the entire United States government…"

Rice launched again into the fabled Battle of Manchester, once more attempting to tie Barrett's actions to his fear of feuding Kentuckians out to kill him. He insisted that his client didn't know Klein and McGovern were federal agents until an old lady in the College Corner yard said, "Them government men are killed."

Rice finished stoutly, if futilely: "The law of self-defense, gentlemen," he said to the jury, "is the oldest law known to mankind. It has been on the books ever since the beginning and it will be there to eternity. Furthermore, no one has a right to take that precious thing the Master gave you. Those agents assaulted him, and they made him kill one of them. They've already put seventy years in prison on his gray hairs, for auto theft, and the hard-boiled prosecutor will come up before you and want to kill him—rub him out. But remember the Bible says, 'Whatever ye judge, that judgment shall be meted out to you.' We ask you in the name of mercy and justice to give the defendant a manslaughter verdict. That's ten years."

Then, said Rice, "He's on the cross. Arms outstretched, and they want you to put the noose around his neck. Give him one last spark of hope. He's already got seventy years." [39]

Judge Baltzell read instructions to the jury and adjourned court until 2:30 p.m. The jury deliberated only from 2:15 p.m. to 3:05 p.m., and they had a verdict. They were so fast, the jurors had to wait another hour to hear the verdict read because Nolan and the prosecution team were still at lunch.

When Barrett was returned to the courtroom, he looked straight ahead as he was wheeled down the long marble corridor from the United States marshal's office by Chief Deputy Marshal Julius J. Wichser and took his place at the table with his attorney. He leaned forward for a minute and whispered to Rice, then settled back in his wheelchair.

When the jurors returned, they looked stern. They appeared to be taking their work seriously. It was, after all, only the second time someone had been tried for the killing of a G-Man under the new statute that made the murder of a government agent a federal offense. The first case was that of a bank robber named John Paul Chase, whom Hoover called "a rat with a patriotic-sounding name." Chase had been present during Baby Face Nelson's shootout with federal agents in which two agents were killed. Chase was ultimately convicted for murder in the spring of 1935 and sentenced to life imprisonment. [40]

A patriotic rat?

John Paul Chase did his undergraduate work as a gopher for Baby Face Nelson—fetching meals and ammunition and carrying messages. Chase's curriculum vitae is somewhat sketchy as to exactly how bad he was, but surely he was bad enough. He was with the Dillinger gang during a 1934 bank heist in which a local policeman was killed, and he was present for the shootout between Baby Face Nelson and federal agents in which two agents died. Chase got away but not for long, and he went on trial in Chicago for murder, where he had the ignominious honor of being the first man charged under the new statute that made the killing of a government agent a federal crime. He was sentenced to life imprisonment and sent to Alcatraz on March 31, 1935. Hoover involved himself in Chase's first parole hearing in 1950, and he even ordered the prison chaplain who supported Chase's parole to be watched. Parole was denied and Chase stayed locked up for another decade before he got out—over Hoover's protests—and went off to California where he worked as a custodian. While at Alcatraz, Chase gained some note for his prison paintings, one of which showed a boat—named the *J.P. Chase*—leaving the island. [41] [42]

Not one of the jurors, who passed just inches away from Barrett's extended feet, looked at him as they walked by. Fred Secrest, the foreman, handed the verdict sheet to the clerk, Albert Sogemeier, who read, "We, the jury, find the defendant George W. Barrett guilty of murder in the first degree." There was no qualification, which meant

The G-man and the Diamond King

that capital punishment was now mandatory. The request for mercy by Barrett's attorney, Rice, had been ignored: Barrett was getting both the seventy years *and* the cross.

None of Barrett's family attended the reading of the verdict. However, Elizabeth Ecker, in whose house Barrett was living in Hamilton, and her 13-year-old granddaughter, Leah, were present. Mrs. Ecker had testified on Barrett's behalf, and she and her granddaughter seemed to be the only ones truly affected by the verdict.[43]

Catharine Klein was not in the courtroom when the verdict was read, nor was Agent McGovern. Cincinnati Agents Earl Connelley, Howard Harris, Robert Klett, J.S. Johnson, and Samuel K. McKee were present, as was the Indianapolis SAC, Harold Reinecke.[44]

The judge set sentencing a week away—December 14—but because of the federal mandate, Barrett's sentence was a foregone conclusion. Barrett, dressed in a gray suit that matched his gray hair and looking like any Midwestern businessman, sat like a block of gray granite, which he had done all through the trial, showing no emotion.

This time, Barrett didn't leave the courtroom by the front; he was wheeled down an inner hallway, out of the public eye and taken to the Marion County Jail where he became an occupant of "the United States row," which got its name after its occupancy over time by federal prisoners. It was, ironically, the first time Barrett had been in jail since his arrest over four months before. He had been housed first at the Fort Hamilton Hospital, and then at the Indianapolis City Hospital.

Director Hoover sent a congratulatory telegram to the United States attorney, Nolan: "I have just been advised of the verdict rendered in the case of George W. Barrett, and I wish to convey to you my deepest appreciation of your tireless efforts not only in preparing the case for trial, but also in the actual trial of same. I think the verdict marks a mile post on the roadway to proper law enforcement in this country, and you are entitled to great credit and commendation for having so aptly presented this case. Not only officially, but personally, I want to extend my congratulations."[45][46]

The trial had lasted just six days, with forty-nine prosecution witnesses and twenty defense witnesses testifying.

In 1935, the film *Top Hat* popularized what would become the Number One song of the year, "Cheek to Cheek," sung by Fred Astaire to Ginger Rogers while they danced. Hearing it could have only brought sadness to Catharine Klein, knowing she would never dance with her husband again. And Barrett, barring a stay of execution, was about to have his last dance, cheek to cheek with the hangman, and he wouldn't be wearing top hat or tails.

ENDNOTES

* The new federal law covering the murder of a government officer provided the death penalty in the district where the crime took place. The law was as follows:

Murder of a Government Officer: U.S. Code, Title 18, Section 253: "Whoever shall kill, as defined in sections 452 and 453 of this title, any United States Marshal or Deputy United States Marshal, Special Agent of the Division of Investigation of the Department of Justice, Post Office Inspector, Secret Service operative, any officer or enlisted man of the Coast Guard, any employee of any United States penal or correctional institution, any officer of the customs or of the internal revenue, any immigrant inspector or any immigration patrol inspector, while engaged in the performance of his official duties, shall be punished as provided under section 454 of this title (May 18, 1934, c. 299, Sec 1, 48 STAT. 789)."

Title 18, section 454 is as follows: "Every person guilty of murder in the first degree shall suffer death. Every person guilty of murder in second-degree shall be imprisoned not less than ten years and may be imprisoned for life. Every person guilty of voluntary manslaughter shall be imprisoned not more than ten years. Every person guilty of involuntary manslaughter shall be imprisoned not more than three years, or fined not exceeding $1,000, or both."

◆ Reinecke, the Indianapolis SAC, made sure Barrett made it to trial.

† Harold H. Reinecke, an Iowan, obtained his law degree from the State University of

The G-man and the Diamond King

Iowa, Iowa City, Iowa, in about 1922. A U.S. Army veteran, he joined the FBI in about 1924 (exact date not available) and by 1934 he was assigned to the Chicago FBI office. Reinecke was present with other agents at the famous shootout in Wisconsin during April, 1934, at the Little Bohemia Lodge involving the Dillinger gang. Dillinger's girlfriend, Evelyn "Billie" Frechette, later testified at her trial that Reinecke struck her during her interrogation. Reinecke denied striking Frechette, telling the court during her harboring trial that he did place his hand under her chin to raise her head so she would look at him during questioning. Frechette was convicted of harboring Dillinger. Reinecke was promoted by Director Hoover to SAC later in 1934, and took charge of the Indianapolis FBI Office that year, with a short stint later in Detroit, then was transferred back to Indianapolis in 1937. He resigned from the FBI in 1939 and became Director of Company Protective Services for the Montgomery-Ward & Company. Reinecke died at Sarasota Memorial Hospital, Sarasota, Florida, in May of 1985. (Courtesy Former Special Agent Larry Wack at *www.historicalgmen. squarespace.com.*)

‡ Howard D. Harris (September 10, 1904–June 25, 1974) was Acting SAC on the day Klein was killed. Harris was a graduate of George Washington University with LL.B. (Bachelor of Laws) and LL.M. (Master of Laws) degrees. After analyzing cases for the Bureau of Standards, Harris joined the BOI on March 3, 1930, his first office of assignment at El Paso, Texas, and after a few months, he was transferred to New York City. In August of 1932 he was reassigned to Cincinnati, Ohio. While in Cincinnati he spent some of his time as head of the Portsmouth, Ohio, office and filling in as Acting SAC in Cincinnati. In November of 1939 he became SAC of the FBI office in Grand Rapids, Michigan. On December 14, 1939, after he was unable to reach Director Hoover by telephone, he typed a resignation letter. In the letter he said that Paul Mooney, Director of Personnel and Public Relations for the Kroger Grocery and Bakery Company in Cincinnati, had made him an offer to become Mooney's assistant. Harris said he regretted leaving the FBI, but

the offer was so generous—and for the good of his family—he had decided to accept the position. He started his new job in Cincinnati in early 1940, retiring from the Kroger Company in 1964 as a Labor Negotiator and resided at 2200 Victory Parkway, in Cincinnati until his death. (Obituary and Harris FBI Personnel File)

§ The Communications Section of the Bureau, established in June of 1935, included four teletype-writers whereby messages could be received and sent to the thirty-seven offices simultaneously or on a singular basis. The new system meant contact could be made with all offices within twelve minutes. (Courtesy former Special Agent Larry Wack at *www.historicalgmen.squarespace.com.*)

|| Earl J. Connelley was born January, 31, 1892, and raised in Columbus, Ohio. In 1917, during the war, Connelley joined the Army as a private, served in the Signal Corps, and was discharged at war's end as a first lieutenant. Connelley studied law and accounting in New York and joined the FBI in January, 1920. In 1927, he was promoted to Special Agent In Charge in St. Louis, and subsequently served in the same capacity in the New York, Chicago, and Cincinnati offices. Throughout his thirty-four-year career, Connelley was involved as an Inspector, and SAC, in many of the most prominent Bureau cases, especially those of the gangster era. Connelley essentially replaced Inspector Sam Cowley in Chicago in late 1934, after Cowley had been killed in action along with SA Herman Hollis. In addition to the major kidnappings, the Dillinger and other cases, Connelley led the raid in Chicago, capturing "Doc" Barker, and subsequently took his men to Florida to capture "Ma" Barker and

The G-man and the Diamond King

her son, Fred. As most know, this attempt led to a gunfight at Ocala, Florida, wherein both Barkers were killed. He retired in 1954, and died at his home in Cincinnati in January, 1957. (Courtesy Former Special Agent Larry Wack at *www.historicalgmen.squarespace.com.*)

⬧ Samuel K. McKee was a graduate of the University of Richmond with a law degree and was a member of the Virginia Bar Association. He served with the FBI from March 31, 1930, until February 28, 1953. He was at the scene of the shooting and killing of Charles Arthur "Pretty Boy" Floyd. He was highly involved

◆ Connelley, Klein's boss in Cincinnati, wears a tie that may have been a bit flashy by agency standards.

in many of the gangster era cases. McKee served as SAC of the Washington Field Office (March 1941–February 1943) and later of the Pittsburgh and Newark field offices in the 1940s and 1950s. After retirement from the FBI, he was employed with the McGregor-Doniger, Inc., as personnel director. He went on to be Director of the Investigative Division of the Wackenhut Corporation in the fall of 1960.

⬧⬧ Will Rogers was a cowboy, actor, vaudevillian, social commentator, philosophical jester, and one of the world's best-known celebrities in the 1920s and 1930s. Wrote *The New York Times* when he died in a plane crash in Alaska in 1935, "He razzed Congress unmercifully, twitted Presidents and Kings, kidded the American public for falling for the blandishments of European borrowers, and he echoed the generally held impression that politicians should do more and talk less."

"I Killed a G-MAN

Now I Hang"

From Barrett's demeanor, he might have been
closing a real estate transaction.

8

George Barrett's last mile

SENTENCING AND APPEAL

On December 11, George Barrett's attorney petitioned the district court for a new trial. He listed what he construed as fourteen errors, which included, among other things, testimony about Barrett's mother, the photographs of Agent Klein's body, even the geography of the trial, which attorney Rice contended should have been held in Liberty, Indiana, the county seat of the place where Klein's death occurred. (Klein and McGovern had been standing in College Corner, Ohio, but Barrett had shot him from twenty-two feet away—and in another state, *West* College Corner, Indiana.)[1]

Then, the same day, Barrett and Rice had an argument, and Rice didn't show up for the December 14 sentencing. The hearing started off with Judge Baltzell asking Barrett if he knew he no longer had an attorney. Barrett said he didn't know.

The judge said Rice had sent him a letter three days before, explaining that he, Rice, had talked to Barrett's sister, who told him Barrett wasn't satisfied with Rice's filing for a new trial, therefore Rice felt he couldn't be of any more service, and he wouldn't be present at the sentence hearing.

Baltzell appointed Will H. Thompson and Fred C. Gause to represent Barrett at sentencing. Thompson was a respected attorney, and Gause was a former Indiana Supreme Court justice and state bar association president.

Then the judge overruled Rice's motion for a new trial. Barrett's demeanor remained unchanged; he sat calmly and demonstrated little emotion. The execution—the first official execution in the county in nearly half a century—was set for March 24, 1936, in the yard of the Marion County Jail in Indianapolis.[2]

"You understand the significance of the verdict that was rendered by the jury last Saturday, do you?" the judge asked.

"I do," Barrett said.

"Have you anything to say as to why judgment should not be pronounced upon that verdict?"

"No," Barrett said. "All I have to say is that I killed Nelson B. Klein in defense of my own life."

"Of course, the jury were the judges of that question, as a question of fact," Judge Baltzell dutifully replied, "and we will have to accept the verdict of the jury upon that very question."

Then the judge said, "It is a hard thing to take away from a person his liberty. That is the hardest task that confronts a judge of any court. And it is much harder, of course, to take away from one the thing we all prize more than anything else in this world—life."

At this, Judge Baltzell paused before continuing. "It is quite possible that you only have a short time to be here. I have been wondering, during the past week, if, in view of that fact, and in view of the statements made by you under oath, whether or not you wanted to change or correct any of those statements at this time. I will now give you that opportunity…"

"Your Honor, I told the truth."

Judge Baltzell outlined the verdict again and the time of the execution, and he ordered Barrett to be held in the Marion County Jail until then.

"As I say," the judge continued, "this is not an easy task and I just want to add one thing, personally—that I hope and pray God will be merciful to you."

Barrett lifted his head and said, "Thank you, your Honor." [3]

Judge Baltzell's remarks were obviously sincere. He did not take lightly the imposing of such a sentence, and he was not unaffected by it. The court historian, Doria Lynch, reported a conversation that occurred between Baltzell and William Steckler in the 1940s, before Steckler became a federal judge. In it, Baltzell said to him, tearfully, "I often wonder whether I will reach heaven as a result of having to pronounce a death sentence."

In another conversation with Steckler, Baltzell said, "Young man, there's one thing I pray you never have to do."

"What's that, Judge Baltzell?"

"I hope and pray that you'll never have to sentence a man to die." [4]

The G-man and the Diamond King

Hanging on

Hanging was thoroughly American, the country's preferred method of execution from the time the Constitution was written until well into the twentieth century, and it's *still* legal in two states, New Hampshire and Washington. For a couple of hundred years or more, the rope held sway (pardon the expression), the problem being that hangmen generally had only so much experience: the condemned might just as easily strangle slowly to death or even be decapitated. Hangings were often festive public spectacles, a bloodthirsty kind of spectator sport for which thousands of spectators turned out, drinking, buying souvenirs, and fighting for the best views. Such events were finally found so offensive that states turned to other methods. The modern era of executions was ushered in by a New York dentist named Albert Southwick who saw an old drunk accidentally—and apparently painlessly— electrocute himself when he stumbled into an electrical generator. The first execution was a few years later, in 1890, when a man named William Kemmler, a convicted murderer, was put to death. That was botched, too: it took eight horrible minutes to kill him, after which inventor George Westinghouse said, "They would have done better with an axe." But the precedent was set, and hangings began to decline. There were few hangings after George Barrett's, and only one since 1977 when Billy Bailey was hanged in Delaware, choosing hanging rather than lethal injection, in which he didn't want to be treated—in his own words—"like a dog put to sleep."[567]

Barrett, as advised by his new attorneys, appealed to the Seventh Circuit Court of Appeals. The appeal outlined, among other items, errors in the admission of evidence, prejudicial cross-examination, and the trial venue. It appeared to cover the same objections as voiced by Rice, Barrett's original attorney. The Seventh Circuit Court of Appeals decided the case on March 17, 1936—a week before the scheduled execution—and affirmed it. The appeals court found unanimously that the district court had not erred.

On January 17, 1936, Barrett wrote a letter to his brother, John, which was discovered in the papers of Judge Baltzell at the Indiana State Library:

Dear brother and family,

I will try to answer your letter as I was glad to hear from you. I hope you are all well. I don't feel very well my arms has been hurting for the last week and my legs are too weak to hold my weight but only about

67 more days to lay here then it will be over no more trouble nor worries. You advise me to forget the worldly goods how would you feel to be going out without leaving a dime a piece for your children it is easy to talk about but it is mighty hard to bear. I love my babies and the others as much as you love yours. When that snake of a Rice (Barrett's attorney) first came to me he said you told him that I must have plenty of money brother where did you think I got it. I sweated blood to get together what little I had. I don't need to repeat the old old story of what went with the big money. God spared my life that afternoon where bullets came all around me it was not my time to go. But in less he intervenes for me I will go shortly after midnight March the 24th. If you remember Pop didn't fear death nor neither do I. But it would make the trip a lot easier to have left my children a few dollars as for my dead body they can bury me or leave me hanging in the jail ward. I written to Rice yesterday, you said he told you he couldn't do any more for me. I didn't ask him to do anything for me for in fact he never done anything, only stole what I had. I have got to get the straight dope on it for he will be sued. I want to know if you gave Sylvania (Barrett's sister) the $740 and the ring or if you gave it to him yourself. To God I had of kept it in my pocket for the man I bought the ring from in St. Louis would've paid me $850 back for it and I could've hired two of the best lawyers in the state for $1000, that would of left me $400. Him telling you if he had of been there the day I was sentenced that the judge would not of appointed any lawyers for me he must take you for a fool for I had five days after I was sentenced to take a Poppers Oath and file an appeal to the US Court of Appeals. Brother I hope your religion sticks to you this time a few other times you sliped back. You tell me to pray without ceasing, read the sixth chapter of St. Matthew it don't say that but I will say this much to you a new light has been born into me and it didn't come from the Baptist Church either. Five months ago yesterday I was shot and the only real friends I have had since then has belonged to the Catholic Church the oldest and the largest on earth. You know that Christ said to Peter upon this rock I will build my church and the gates of hell shall not prevail against it. That was 1900 years ago the Baptist is 700 years old. John D, I had in my trunk a new tie that I got two years ago from Little Jack please give it to Finley and you can have my overcoat but I want Carlos to have the watch let me hear from you. I am writing to Sylvania to learn just how things were handled and to find out so I can sue him for the return of my ring he brought a note for me to sign that she had already signed for $600 said that was his fee well I am so tired and my arms hurt so I will close. Love Brother (we have all sinned and come short of the glory of God)

THE EXECUTION

The last previous execution in Marion County, Indiana, had taken place on April 18, 1886, when Robert Phillips, a black man, was hanged for killing his wife. At some point, Indiana law was changed, and it allowed for execution only by electric chair while the federal government's punishment was death by hanging.*

The G-man and the Diamond King

The method of execution proved problematic for the court because it had no gallows. So the marshals located Phil Hanna, an Indiana farmer and stock breeder who, shocked by a hanging that had gone awry, had undertaken a study of hanging's methodology. In the process, he had inadvertently made himself into a man known as "the Human Hangman." He volunteered his services, never accepting pay, and he seemed genuinely concerned that, should hanging be used, then it should be used as humanely as possible. His was a personal crusade to make execution by hanging painless.[8]

Hanna found a gallows in Illinois, took it apart, brought it to Indianapolis, and put it back together in the courtyard of the Marion jail. His wife made the hood for Barrett.[9]

Hangman Hanna

Phil Hanna was a legend in a most peculiar craft—the public hanging. And even so, he was, by most accounts, an unusual advocate. For Hanna practiced reluctantly, and what he was really after was a painless exit for the condemned. This personal crusade seemed to have originated when Hanna, as a young man, witnessed an execution by an inexperienced hangman in which a man strangled slowly to death. He was deeply disturbed by what he had seen (one biography said he suffered from algophobia, the abnormal fear of pain, although with Hanna it was the pain of others rather than his own, as though this pain had been transferred to *him*). "It is not a nice thing to see a man die," he said, "or to have a part in executing him. My point is that if men are to be put to death, it should be done mercifully. I would rather supervise a hanging and have it done correctly than to attend to my farm chores and read that another hanging has been bungled by an inexperienced sheriff." And so he began to study the methodology of hanging, becoming a sought-after consultant across the country. He tested weights and heights, practiced with plow lines and straw dummies, and commissioned a special rope made of soft fibers which he kept in a moisture-proof box. He taught the condemned about a conduct that minimized their fear and suffering, and sometimes he personally adjusted the knot on the noose. Eight months after George Barrett's hanging, Hanna was present in Owensville, Kentucky, for the hanging of Rainey Bethea—said to be the last person publicly executed in America. By all accounts, Hanna was ecstatic to finally be out of work.[12] [13] [14]

Phil Hanna found a gallows in Illinois and re-assembled it in Indianapolis for Barrett's execution.

A few days before the execution, Barrett abruptly stood up in his cell and declared that he was going to kill himself—and anyone who tried to stop him. He suggested that he would grind up his glass eye and swallow it, or use his eye glasses. Marshal Wichser and Dr. Dwyer persuaded him to give up both items. No additional security had been placed around his cell at night because of Barrett's paralyzed legs, but because of his recent outbursts those in charge added an additional guard.[10]

On March 22, workers were still completing the gallows in the jail yard; it was hidden by a tent to keep prying eyes out. Barrett could hear the banging and said to one of the guards, "I'd five times rather die that way than be electrocuted."

While re-assembling the gallows, Hanna and Barrett had a conversation in Barrett's cell about the hanging, with Hanna appearing more nervous than Barrett.

"What part do you do in this?" Barrett said, dunking toast in his coffee.

"Well," Hanna said, clearing his throat, "I tie the noose and adjust it around the neck."

"What do you mean?" Barrett asked calmly.

"I mean the rope," Hanna said in a very low tone.

"Oh yes, yes, the rope. I didn't understand you."

Barrett went on dunking his toast, over the noisy sounds of the hammering outside. Hanna then asked Barrett if he would be able to stand on the scaffold.

"I'll do my best," Barrett said.[11]

Barrett also gave a deathbed interview to a magazine writer named Victor Rankin. "I hang tomorrow," he told Rankin, and Rankin wrote that Barrett "spoke dully, as if his soul had already fled and the voice came from the wasted shell of a man that had been. It gave one the horrible feeling that he was interviewing death itself."

The following was a letter written by Laura Barrett Crawford (Barrett's cousin) on behalf of her mother, Orleana Bowling Barrett (Barrett's aunt), to Barrett sometime in the first half of March, 1936:

The G-man and the Diamond King

Dear George:

I will write you a few lines to let you know I got your letter and I was glad to hear from you once more. I am very sorry things are like they are. But God knows everything and will give justice, and I am thankful to know that you feel the way you do. Keep on asking God to be with you and give your whole heart to him, and he will take care of you.

George, mother is here with me and will make her home with me as long as she lives, and I will take care of her as good as I can. John said to give you his best regards and deepest sympathy. I wish there was something we could do, but I don't reckon there is. If there is anything you want to write to us, do so.

George, Lucy said Rachel told her that she put her trust all in God the morning before she died. Mother said the last time you left her, she felt worse about you than she ever did, felt like she wouldn't never see you again. But she said she hoped to meet you in Heaven. She will be 79 the 18th of March.

Well I will close for this time. Wish I could say more. From your cousin and family.

Goodbye and may God bless you [15]

Father McShane: he gave Barrett the church's last rites.

On the last day of January, Barrett received the sacraments of baptism and communion from Reverend John Francis McShane, pastor at St. Bridget's Catholic Church in Indianapolis. Father McShane had visited Barrett daily, providing him with his sole source of comfort by reading Scripture. Father McShane praised Barrett's intelligence and indicated that Barrett had "shown a broad knowledge of religious history and had a unique choice of words." [16]

On March 22, the Reverend McShane administered the last rites sacrament to Barrett in the presence of his sister Sylvania and special guard D.S. Rivera. His last meal was T-bone steak, French fried potatoes, stewed corn, lettuce salad, and coffee, provided by a local restaurant. He ate half and gave the rest to a stray jailhouse cat. [17]

On March 23, the day before the execution, people began gathering on the Alabama Street side of the Marion County Jail. A drizzling rain in the morning didn't keep them away. Traffic was so heavy that a squad of traffic police had to be added to keep vehicles moving. After the crowd become so heavy they blocked the street in front of the jail, Sheriff Otto Ray† made arrangements with federal authorities, allowing spectators to file past the tented scaffold in the jail yard. It was estimated that 4,000 to 5,000 people passed by the scaffold, including many women.[18][19]

Death Cell Confession of the Midwest's Most Infamous Slayer

THE last shadows of the setting sun filtered through the steel bars of the hospital cell and cast eerie shadows on the whitewashed stone walls. The wasted figure on the steel cot turned slowly toward the narrow door beyond which I sat with Sheriff Ray. Near us two United States deputy marshals paced silently up and down within earshot of the prisoner. Faintly on the chill March air came the steady clop, clop of the carpenter's hammer driving the last nails in the scaffold upon which the man facing us was to hang sometime between midnight and dawn of March 24. Then George Barrett, Kentucky feudist, mother murderer and most deadly of all gunmen would pay the supreme penalty for the murder of a G-man.

"I will hang tomorrow." He spoke dully as if his soul had already fled and the voice came from the wasted shell of a man that had been. It gave one the horrible feeling that he was interviewing death itself.

"There's little time left for me to atone for the crimes I have committed or the wrongs I have done in this world. It is too late for me to ask forgiveness of anyone save God. This I have done, and I feel that I have a through ticket to heaven. I want to leave this world bearing no grudge against anyone. I want a clear conscience. I want to meet my mother and my sister Rachel in heaven and tell them why I killed them. No man can say that there isn't a hell on earth. I've suffered its tortures a thousand times before my time finally came to go, before I learned that crime doesn't pay. Now it's too late for me to

Leaving the hospital after this amazing interview with George Barrett, opposite page, Sheriff Ray examines the notes held by the author. Below, crowds outside stare at covered scaffold.

An Interview with
GEORGE W. BARRETT
By
VICTOR P. RANKIN

31

◆ Barrett made headlines, many of them sensational, across the country.

The G-man and the Diamond King

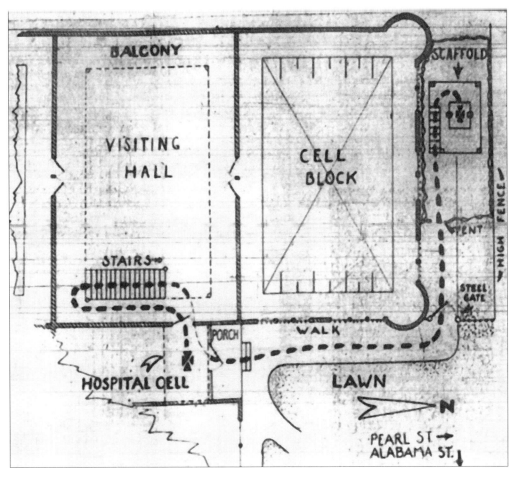

This drawing of the Marion County Jail shows where Barrett was executed.

Barrett called a press conference, which was held outside his prison cell. "Boys," he said, "I called you here to tell you I hold no malice toward anyone. I think everyone connected to this thing did his duty. I can't leave here hating anyone. I have nothing against you. When I leave, I know I've got a through-ticket to Heaven. You can't get to Heaven hating anyone. I know I'm going to Heaven, and that I'm going to meet my mother there." Barrett went on to say that he had confessed his sins to Father McShane and converted to Catholicism.[20]

At 11:30 p.m., Alabama Street was still packed with pedestrians, despite the rain that had been falling since early evening. Inside the yard were some government employees and their families. They'd had enough pull to get into the jail but not the tent, and they stood on either side of two lines of deputies and policemen between the jail and the tent. The privileged few—forty or fifty witnesses, officials, and news reporters—sat on wooden folding chairs, as though they were awaiting a lecture or a solemn concert of some kind.[21]

George Barrett's last mile

Barrett's death march began at 11:50, led by an *Indianapolis Star* reporter—and devout Catholic—named Horace Coats, who carried a lighted candle in each hand. Barrett, holding a crucifix, was carried from his cell on a stretcher, supported by four deputy marshals. They proceeded up through a coal chute, but midway between the cell and tent, a woman in the crowd fainted and sprawled across the walkway; they stepped over her and walked on.[22][23]

Once in the tent, Barrett was carried up the thirteen steps of the scaffold. His eyes were closed, and he gave no sign of life even when he was lifted from the stretcher by two deputy marshals. He was dressed in a pair of Marion County Sheriff Otto Ray's white pajamas, wishing to save his only suit for burial.

He was asked by Sheriff Ray if he had any last words, and he responded weakly, "Nothing, nothing at all."

There was a prayer in Latin by Father McShane, then Hanna placed the noose around Barrett's throat, gave the rope a few tugs, and placed the hood over his head. As the tension increased, someone in the crowd vomited, the retching echoing repulsively within the tent.[24]

At 12:01 a.m. on March 24, 1936, Hanna stepped back and raised his arm, then dropped it in silence. Arthur "Charley" Reeves, deputy sheriff, who was only five feet tall and a former circus trapeze artist, had volunteered for the job nobody wanted. Reeves, standing at the bottom of the scaffold, pulled the lever that released the trapdoor. It was exactly two minutes past midnight.[25][26]

Ten minutes later, Barrett was pronounced dead (the official time of death was 12:12 a.m.), and the body was taken to the jail garage and prepared for burial. Barrett was buried that same day at the Holy Cross Cemetery in Indianapolis. Reverend McShane conducted services at the gravesite. A small group attended, including the following: a church choir; deputy United States marshals; Barrett's sister, Mrs. Sylvania Woods of Lockland, Ohio; and his brother, John D. Barrett of College Corner, Ohio. Sylvania spent most of Barrett's last day with him. John had car trouble and did not arrive until after Barrett was pronounced dead.[27]

The U.S. marshal's office in Indianapolis wanted Marion County to pay the $75 cost of burying Barrett, as he was a WWI veteran with an honorable discharge. The county dismissed the request because Barrett had not been a resident for a year before his death. The federal government ended up paying the bill as well as the hanging cost, which totaled $245.26. This included expenses for repair and transportation of the scaffold; expenses of George Phillip Hanna, the hangman; and two assistants.[28]

The G-man and the Diamond King

CASE CLOSED

The various indictments charging Barrett with violation of the National Motor Vehicle Theft Act—there were at least four, from Ohio to California—were dismissed after Barrett's death. Director Hoover told the Indianapolis SAC, Dowd, to obtain all the case exhibit items from United States Attorney Nolan and send them to the Bureau. Nolan had asked about donating Barrett's license plates to the Indiana State Police Museum, which had just opened, but Hoover didn't like the idea; he reasoned that none of the items should go to the police museum because federal agents had handled the Barrett investigation. The plates, instead, went to the Chief Clerk's office for destruction.

The clothes worn by Agent Klein the night he was killed—used as an exhibit at the trial—were destroyed by the Indianapolis FBI office, and so was the hand towel stamped "Seybold Hotel," which Barrett used to hide his gun.

Barrett's two guns— the .45-caliber Colt revolver Bisley model, serial # 3168989, and the Colt New Series .38 caliber WCF revolver—went to the FBI laboratory to be placed in its firearms collection.

The FBI file 26-HQ-38858 investigating George Barrett was officially closed in August of 1936. The title had gone through numerous additions with the following being the most complete at the time of closing:

TITLE: GEORGE W. BARRETT, with aliases George W. Ball, James L. Black, George W. Martin, James L. Anderson, George H. Clark, J.D. Long, J.D. Little, George Smith, White Burnett; Nelson B. Klein(deceased); Edna Parrott–victim.

CHARACTER OF CASE: National Motor Vehicle Theft Act, Murder of Special Agent Nelson B. Klein, Unlawful Flight to Avoid Prosecution, White Slave Traffic Act.

The file itself was as emotionless as Barrett had appeared during his trial, as if he had known that his life had been terribly misspent and now it was over.

George Barrett's last mile

END NOTES

* "The modern method of judicial hanging is called the long drop. Those planning the execution calculate the drop distance required to break the subject's neck, based on his or her weight, height and build. The aim is to get the body moving quickly enough after the trap door opens to produce between 1,000 and 1,250 foot-pounds of torque on the neck when the noose jerks tight. This distance can be anywhere from five to nine feet. The jolt to the neck at the end of the drop is enough to break or dislocate a neck bone called the axis, which in turn should sever the spinal cord. In some cases, the hangman jerks up on the rope at the precise moment when the drop is ending in order to facilitate the breakage. This is the ideal situation in a long drop. When the neck breaks and severs the spine, blood pressure drops to nothing in about a second, and the subject loses consciousness. Brain death then takes several minutes, and complete death can take more than fifteen or twenty minutes, but the person at the end of the rope most likely does not feel or experience anything." ("How does death by hanging work?" *http://health. howstuffworks.com/diseases-conditions/death-dying/death-by-hanging.htm*)

† Otto Ray grew up on the South side of Indianapolis, dropped out of school at age 10 to work as a bricklayer's helper and a plumber's helper at $2.50 a week and self-educated himself by reading English dictionaries and copying them into a tablet. He joined the Army in 1917 during WWI and trained recruits, later becoming an Indianapolis police captain and sheriff of Marion County. His family's farm on Michigan Road in Indianapolis became the Otto Ray Animal Shelter, which found homes for thousands of dogs, and it eventually became the Indianapolis Humane Society shelter. (*Obituary from the Indianapolis-Marion County Public Library*)

‡ "The modern noose is prepared in accordance with a procedure laid down in a U.S. Army manual, from thirty feet of three-quarters inch to one inch diameter rope, boiled

The G-man and the Diamond King

to take out stretch and tendency to coil. It is formed into six coils, then waxed, soaped or greased to ensure that the knot slides easily. The knot is normally placed beneath the prisoner's left ear and the noose drawn fairly tight. It was realized that it was necessary to take out the stretch from the rope to prevent the prisoner bouncing up again in the trap, as happened in earlier times. In some states this was done by dropping a bag of sand of approximately the same weight as the prisoner and then leaving it suspended for some hours prior to the execution." ("Hanged by the neck until you are dead! (USA)," http://www.capitalpunishmentuk.org/hanging.html)

George Barrett's last mile

The Kleins in a pastoral family moment.

9 The Director takes care of his own

Early in 1936, Brent Spence, the New Deal politician from Fort Thomas, Kentucky, who would soon become one of the most powerful members of the United States Congress, took a very special interest in Catharine Klein's misfortune, even to introducing a new bill on her behalf.

Then Director Hoover wrote Mrs. Klein on January 9, telling her that the attorney general had submitted to the House and Senate claims committees copies of a bill to provide compensation to her for the death of her husband, and that he, Hoover, was deeply interested in the matter.[1]

On January 28, Hoover again wrote Mrs. Klein, enclosing a copy of "Bill H.R. 10575"—introduced by Congressman Spence—which just days before had been brought to the House of Representatives on her behalf. Hoover said he was hopeful that Congress would act favorably on the bill. Mrs. Klein conveyed to Director Hoover her appreciation.[2]

At the end of March, R. Whitley, the New York office SAC, sent a letter to Hoover marked "personal and confidential." In it, Whitley spoke of being visited by Agent Klein's father, Harry A. Klein. Mr. Klein was still greatly upset over his son's death, and he was calling on Whitley to talk about his deceased boy, with whom Whitley had worked in the Charlotte office years before.

Mr. Klein said that Catharine Klein had never recovered from the shock of Nelson's unexpected death, that she was still residing at the same address where they had previously lived, and that he, Harry Klein, was trying to get her to move. He felt certain that a change of surroundings would be beneficial to her.

121

Mr. Klein went on to say that he would very much like to meet with Director Hoover some day in Washington, D.C., or New York City. Whitley told Mr. Klein that the Director would be pleased to meet with him.[3]

On May 11, 1936, Hoover sent Mrs. Klein a letter telling her that on May 4, Bill H.R. 10575 had been signed into law by President Franklin D. Roosevelt, allocating $5,000 annually for her. The Director said it would be necessary for Mrs. Klein to make a written application to the secretary of the treasury for the amount granted, and he went on to say that if he could be of any further assistance, she should not hesitate to telephone.[4]

The man, the bridge

Brent Spence was a good friend for Catharine Klein to have. When her husband died in 1935, Spence was not yet the legendary power broker he would become, but he was on his way. As Newport city solicitor, he never lost a suit and in 1930, he was elected to the U.S. Congress—then won re-election fifteen more times. He was an ardent New Dealer and when plans to expand Lunken Airport went awry, Spence's loyalty to President Roosevelt helped get the new Cincinnati airport built—in Kentucky. He pushed for urban renewal and as chair of the House Banking Committee helped write some of the country's foremost financial legislation, which included federal mortgage insurance. He was a big—6-foot-3, 230 pounds—man but his size was offset by his manner, which was often shy and low-key. Today, he is best known as a bridge—the Brent Spence, a double-decker that carries interstate traffic across the Ohio (the bridge's approach—and the downtown Cincinnati skyline—was featured

for years on the soap opera The Edge of Night). He didn't want his name on it, though, and he said it should be named after John F. Kennedy, who was assassinated three days before the bridge was to open. The Kentucky governor, Bert Combs, thought Kennedy's name would appear on other structures, and that the bridge was Spence's. The Congressman died four years later, in 1967, at age 92.[5][6]

◆ Remembered for his bridge, Brent Spence was much more.

The G-man and the Diamond King

Mrs. Klein wrote Hoover on May 16 to tell him that Congressman Spence had sent a letter of application for her to sign, and he would file it with the secretary of the treasury on her behalf. Mrs. Klein thanked the Director for assisting her and assured him that it would be of great help to her in the education and welfare of her children. She also said she had been given great pleasure while reading of the Director's recent success in rounding up and capturing "all of the kidnapping gangs." At the bottom of her letter, in his own hand, Hoover requested that Mrs. Klein's name be placed on the FBI's mailing list (for sending out notices, Christmas cards, etc.)[7].

On July 14, Mrs. Klein wrote the Director that she was spending a month at her former husband's family residence in New Jersey and that any mail could be forwarded to her at that address. She said she had received a check for $5,000 and again thanked Hoover for his assistance. She said she had received a copy of the Director's most recent radio talk for which she was very grateful. "You are doing such fine work," she wrote, "and I am and always will be interested in the Bureau. My only hope is that my boys will grow up to be as fine as the men in the Bureau."[8]

Then in September, the New York office SAC, Whitley, sent a personal letter to Hoover, telling him that Harry Klein had telephoned the office and was eager to talk to the Director, although it would be impossible for him to go to Washington for that purpose. He had asked when the Director would be in New York, so that he might meet him there.

Whitley reported that Klein appeared to be considerably upset and worried about Catharine Klein. She had continued on in the residence with her children, and from her window she could observe her husband's grave in the cemetery; and Klein said she was in serious mental condition as a result of her continued grief. Mr. Klein said again that he felt it was very important that she move her residence and to secure employment so that she might occupy her time.

Hoover said he would be very glad to talk with Mr. Klein upon his next visit to New York City.[9]

Two days before Christmas, Assistant Director Tolson sent a memorandum to the Director about a recent executive conference where assistance to employees in need during the Christmas season was discussed. It was noted that while at the present time the widows of various agents who have lost their lives in Bureau service were receiving appropriate attention, in a few years the children of these agents would reach an age whereby they might desire to attend school or college and that the Bureau should be on alert to provide whatever assistance was possible. The status of Mrs. Klein was discussed, with the members deciding to have the Cincinnati SAC discreetly ascertain her present financial condition in order to determine any material items or toys the children might need, and that arrangements then could be made to have them delivered in time for Christmas.[10]

On December 27, Inspector T. D. Quinn, in a memorandum to Tolson, said that the Cincinnati office SAC had been in contact with Mrs. Klein, who had been visiting her family in Mount Vernon, Ohio, during Christmas. She appeared to be living comfortably and the children seemed to have everything they desired. The SAC had said to Mrs. Klein more than once that the Director would act favorably upon any request she might make for employment. She said that she could not at this time make up her mind just what she wished to do.

The Cincinnati SAC indicated that Agent Klein apparently had quite a bit of insurance, the exact amount unknown, and that while Mrs. Klein had nothing elaborate in the way of a home, it was comfortable. The SAC's wife frequently called upon Mrs. Klein and they would go on shopping tours, and during these times the SAC's wife noticed that neither Mrs. Klein nor the children appeared to be lacking financial resources.[11]

In the autumn of 1938, Mrs. Klein wrote Director Hoover saying that she had received a couple of his speeches, which she enjoyed reading very much. She also received *The Investigator** which she found interesting, as it contained many names she knew. She asked what a subscription cost, indicated that the children were fine, and hoped that the Director was enjoying good health. In the margins of the letter, Hoover made a notation that paying for *The Investigator* was not necessary.[12]

On December 8, Director Hoover wrote, thanking her for her letter and that he was happy *The Investigator* proved of interest to her. There was no subscription charge for it, and it would be sent to her as long as she wanted, "since we of the FBI still regard you as being part of our organization." He was glad the children were in good health and was pleased they were progressing nicely.[13]

In the spring of 1939, the Indianapolis SAC, Herold H. Reinecke, wrote the Director that he had visited Mrs. Klein at her home in Danville, Ohio. The Director was pleased to learn that Mrs. Klein enjoyed reading the various publications of the FBI that had been sent by the Director. The Director had enclosed an autographed photograph with one of his letters, as Mrs. Klein had requested through SAC Reinecke. "In the event an occasion arises where I can be of assistance," Hoover had written her, "I want you to be sure to call upon me."[14]

In June of 1944, Mrs. Klein wrote the Director under a new name—she was now Catharine Wright, having married Harry S. Wright of Mt. Vernon, Ohio, on May 24. Mrs. Wright thanked Director Hoover for sending her the April issue of *The Investigator*,

The G-man and the Diamond King

which honored the memory of Agent Klein and other agents killed in the line of duty. She said that Nelson Jr. had graduated from Danville High School in May and intended to enlist in the Navy when he turned 18; Richard was to be a junior in high school, and Barbara Ann would enter junior high in the next school year.

Mrs. Wright said that the children wanted to finish school in Mount Vernon, and she understood that re-marrying automatically terminated her federal compensation, but she wanted to know from the Director what effect her marital status would have on the children.[15]

Director Hoover answered her letter in July, telling her that her children, within certain limitations, would continue to receive benefits under the Compensation Act. He suggested that she communicate directly with the U.S. Employee Compensation Commission in New York and advise them of her change in marital status. (Her compensation ceased at the end of May, although the children would, until each turned 18, receive semi-monthly checks for slightly more than $30—the equivalent of about $400 in today's dollars.)

The Director congratulated Catharine on her marriage and was pleased to learn of the progress of the children. His letter ended, "With best wishes for your future happiness, I remain sincerely yours, John Edgar Hoover, Director."[16]

ENDNOTES

* The Investigator was first printed on April 4, 1932, as a result of an employee suggestion and was sponsored by the Bureau of Investigation Athletic Association, which would later become the FBI Recreation Association (FBIRA). The first issue appeared on May 9, 1932, and was one page, titled "Bureau Bulletin." It was first mainly about sports but in its second year it had interesting cases, sketches, and appeared monthly. In 1935 it started to contain photographs and by the 1950s, photos and stories about employees were prevalent. In October 1978, it became an official FBI publication and hence was no longer available to former employees. It is no longer published in print format but is located on the FBI's internal website.

The Director takes care of his own

Nelson and Catharine Klein are seen here as though
George Barrett would not intrude into their lives.

10 Epilogue

Agent Klein was the first and only FBI Agent killed in the line of duty in the Tri-state. He lived in northern Kentucky, worked in the Cincinnati FBI Office, and was killed in Indiana. The trial of his killer was the first murder trial ever held in the U.S. District Court for the Southern District of Indiana. The jury returned a verdict in fifty minutes, and the government obtained just the second conviction under the new 1934 law that made killing a federal officer a capital offense. The man who killed Klein, George Barrett, had been indicted, tried, convicted, sentenced and executed in a span of seven months, a fitting fate for a career criminal.

The memory and sacrifice of Agent Klein lives on: his name is inscribed on the wall of the National Law Enforcement Officers Memorial in Washington, D.C.; in the video Wall of Honor—deceased agents killed in the line of duty—which is found in every FBI field office; and on a memorial plaque located in the Cincinnati FBI Office lobby. In addition, the FBI Indianapolis office is located at 8825 Nelson B. Klein Parkway, and his gravesite stone in Evergreen Cemetery in Southgate, Kentucky, is embedded with an FBI badge.

Nelson Bernard Klein—April 3, 1898 to August 16, 1935

On August 16, 2013, on the seventy-eighth anniversary of Klein's death, a dedication was held at the Cincinnati Office of the FBI during which the SFSAFBI, Cincinnati Chapter, dedicated a twenty-three-inch by thirty-two-inch plaque to the Cincinnati FBI office commemorating Agent Klein's sacrifice. Eight members of Klein's family attended, along with active and retired FBI personnel and a number of local dignitaries. The dedication was a collaborative effort between the Cincinnati FBI and the SFSAFBI.

💎 Klein's name is on the memorial wall in Washington.

The inscription on the plaque reads:

Nelson B. Klein

1898–1935

Served Honorably

December 10, 1926 to August 16, 1935

Special Agent Klein was born on April 3, 1898, in New York City and served his country as a sergeant in the U.S. Army, 69th infantry, Fighting Irish, New York National Guard, during World War I.

On Aug. 16, 1935, he and Special Agent Donald C. McGovern learned that a suspected car thief, George W. Barrett, was visiting his brother in College Corner, IN. Barrett, a convicted criminal known as the "Diamond King," ran a scam in which he stole rental cars, altered them slightly, and then sold them as used cars. As part of the operation, he transported them across state lines, which violated the National Motor Vehicle Theft Act and made his crime a federal offense.

Klein and McGovern drove to Barrett's brother's residence, spotted Barrett near an automobile and, fearing he was about to escape, identified themselves and called on him to surrender. Klein noticed that Barrett was wearing a short sleeve shirt and falsely assumed that he was unarmed. During the ensuing chase, Barrett turned toward the agents and opened fire. Klein and McGovern returned fire, Klein firing 10 shots.

The G-man and the Diamond King

Klein was struck with five bullets shot from Barrett's revolver, and died at the scene. Barrett was wounded in both legs and was transported to Fort Hamilton Hospital, where he spent five days recovering.

In 1934, the U.S. Congress had enacted a law making the killing of a federal officer a capital offense. Barrett received the death penalty on December 7, 1935. On March 24, 1936, Barrett was executed by hanging in Marion County, IN.

Klein left a wife, Catharine, and three children, Nelson Jr., Richard C., and Barbara Ann. He was buried in Evergreen Cemetery, Southgate, KY. Nelson Jr. would later become a Special Agent with the FBI; he died in a traffic accident in 1969. Barbara joined the FBI as a support employee and was assigned to Director J. Edgar Hoover's office.

Nelson Klein in a tranquil moment at home.

On June 7, 2012, the Cincinnati Division building was dedicated in memory of Special Agent Nelson Klein, in honor of his ultimate sacrifice.

George W. Barrett—February 7, 1887, to March 24, 1936

Barrett told his relatives a short while before he was executed that they should "believe in God and obey the law and they would never end up in his position." Barrett converted to Catholicism a few weeks before he was executed and received the sacrament of Reconciliation.

Barrett believed that he was going to heaven and would be with his mother and sister Rachel and could explain to them why he killed them. Barrett is buried in an unmarked grave at Holy Cross and St. Joseph Cemetery, Indianapolis, Indiana, Section 9 – G, lot 1027. Sylvania Wood (sister) was listed as next of kin on the cemetery's registration card.

Donald Conrad McGovern—July 21, 1905, to April 13, 1966

The youthful-looking agent, age 30 in 1935, was transferred from Cincinnati, Ohio, to St. Paul, Minnesota, after the incident. He reported for duty at St. Paul, Minnesota, on September 9, 1935, and was described by his supervisor as being somewhat nervous, most likely from the shootout.

On December 12, 1935, United States Attorney Nolan sent a letter to Director Hoover advising him of how pleased he was with the remarkable work of the FBI in the Barrett investigation. Agent McGovern and the other Cincinnati agents were mentioned as having exemplary witness-stand presence. Nolan indicated that this roused the admiration of all who saw and heard them in the courtroom. Attorney Nolan mentioned to Indianapolis SAC H.H. Reinecke that the FBI Agents "are fine, damn good men."[1]

On December 13, 1935, Nolan sent a letter to McGovern which stated, "You will recall that I said to you before the trial that the success of this prosecution would depend largely upon the impression which your testimony made upon the jury. I have never seen or heard a more convincing witness than you were, and I feel now that your manner and bearing on the witness stand and your splendid presentation of the facts to the court and jury was of controlling influence."[2]

However, even after receiving commendations for his participation in the Barrett case, McGovern's luck didn't hold. Early in 1936, while traveling in rural Minnesota to conduct an insurance investigation, his car struck some ice and he went through a guard rail into a farmer's field. He hired the farmer to extricate the Bureau vehicle with a team of horses, and he felt the damage was so negligible he didn't make a report with the agency when he returned to St. Paul.

Donald McGovern rushed to his partner's rescue but too late.

When the St. Paul SAC asked about the vehicle, McGovern said it was in the garage for $65 worth of repairs, which he was paying. On January 26, 1936, Inspector T.D. Quinn recommended to Assistant Director Tolson that McGovern should receive a fifteen-day suspension without pay for failing to report the Bureau automobile accident.

The G-man and the Diamond King

On January 31, 1936, Director Hoover requested McGovern to submit his resignation from the FBI. Hoover said this action was being taken because of McGovern's unsatisfactory development as a special agent, his carelessness in connection with the loss of government property (weapon), and his failure to report an accident involving a Bureau automobile.

After he left the FBI, McGovern practiced law in Washington, D.C., and during WWII, he served in the United States Army Air Corps as an intelligence officer. He served in North Africa, Italy, and Sicily, rising to the rank of Lieutenant Colonel. For his service he received the WWII Victory Medal, American Campaign Medal, European African Middle Eastern Service Medal, and Honorable Service Lapel Button WWII. [3]

On February 22, 1947, in Los Angeles, McGovern married Evelyn Marie Hursh, who was from Olympia, Washington. They had three children: John Michael, Michael Donald, and Patricia Marie.

McGovern died of a massive heart attack while working at the law office of Hodges, McGovern, and Shelton in Santa Monica. McGovern was a member of SFSAFBI and the Washington, D.C., New York, and California Bar Associations. He is buried at Woodlawn Cemetery in Santa Monica. He was described by his son Michael as an inventor and a proponent of higher education who was very gregarious and courageous.

Catharine Isabella (Cox) Klein—March 8, 1897, to April 22, 1987

Her son Richard described her as 5-foot-7 with red hair and recalled that she was always very formal in entertaining, using the good china and adhering to the teachings of Emily Post.* Richard thought that his father, Nelson, was the love of her life, even though she remarried. She had great respect for Nelson as a man and would often say, "What would your father think?" when the children were up to mischief. She would also tell her children, "Make your father proud." She described Nelson as a quiet man who was a good listener. [4]

She married her second husband, Harry S. Wright of Mount Vernon, Ohio, on May 27, 1944. She developed Parkinson's disease late in life but was still able to cook, pumpkin pie being one of her favorites. She died at age 90 in Palm Bay, Florida, with both of her husbands, older son and daughter preceding her in death. [5]

Nelson "Bud" Klein Jr.— September 23, 1926, to May 30, 1969

He was born in Atlantic City, New Jersey, and moved at an early age with his family to Danville, Ohio. He graduated from Danville High School where he starred in football and

The Klein children as they were not long before their father's death.

basketball. He served at the Naval Station Great Lakes with the U.S. Navy during WWII. After naval service he attended the Ohio State University, graduating in 1950. On July 6, 1951, he was sworn in as a federal probation officer at Cleveland, Ohio. He became an FBI Special Agent in July 1955 and served until 1969, when he was killed in a traffic accident at Statesboro, Georgia, while on official FBI business. His wife, Betty, resides in Mt. Vernon, Ohio, and they had three children, William Richard, Thomas Edward, and Sue Ann.[67]

Richard Cox Klein—November 3, 1928– He graduated from high school in 1946, enlisted in the U.S. Army, and was stationed in Korea for thirteen months. Afterward, he attended the Ohio State University on the GI Bill, graduating in 1952 with a degree in Agricultural Science. He worked for the U.S. Conservation Service for a few years, Gerber Baby Food, the Burroughs Corporation, then tried his hand as a real estate agent. He retired as a food inspector with the U.S. Department of Agriculture in 1989 with twenty-five years of federal service. He lives in St. Cloud, Florida, with his wife, Barbara; they have three grown children.

Barbara Ann Klein Fleischmann—April 1, 1932, to July 29, 1978
She was the little blonde-haired four-year-old girl wearing a yellow dress who sat on her mother's lap during the trial and was photographed afterward in her Southgate neighborhood with Hamilton, a white Persian cat who was a neighborhood fixture. In 1936, the Director learned about Barbara being quarantined with scarlet fever and wrote his sympathies.

Barbara was employed by the federal government in Washington, for twenty-five years, and lived in Maryland. First employed by the FBI and assigned to Director Hoover's office, she later worked in the Census Bureau. She died at the age of 46 in Mt. Vernon, Ohio. Her daughter, Kathryn Fleischman Stemmer, lives in Anderson Township, Ohio, and is a teacher.[8]

The G-man and the Diamond King

END NOTES

'For most of the twentieth century, Emily Post was America's authority on what the *New York Times* called "matters of social good form." Her basic rule, which underlay all others, was that "no one should do anything that can either annoy or offend the sensibilities of others." Her book, *Etiquette*, was published in 1922, and was in its eighty-ninth edition when she died in 1960; *Emily Post's Etiquette* is still in print, edited first by her granddaughter-in-law and now by her great-granddaughter-in-law. ("Emily Post Is Dead Here at 86," *The New York Times*, September 27, 1960)

Chronology

The following is a Summary of Agency Events that occurred during Nelson Klein's career (1926-1935):

○ October 1926—The Fugitive Division of the Bureau is created.

Cases for the year include that of Gerald Chapman, "The Gentleman Bandit" (and the first Public Enemy Number One), and his partner-in-crime George "Dutch" Anderson, who rob a New York mail truck of $2.4 million; the investigation and conviction of John Worthington, "The Wolf of La Salle Street" and con man extraordinaire; and the murder of Special Agent Edward C. Shanahan, the first Special Agent killed in the line of duty. He is shot in a Chicago garage by auto thief Martin Durkin when Shanahan tries to apprehend him without waiting for his backup men who are on lunch break.

During 1926, the number of Special Agents in the field is reduced by sixteen.

○ September 15, 1927—The first Manual of Investigation—covering rules and regulations on investigations—is issued to Agents, Supervisors and SACs.

○ June 30, 1927—Bankruptcy cases investigated increase 100 percent over previous year.

Important cases resulting in convictions are that of Roy and Ray DeAutremont, notorious fugitives from justice since October, 1923. Their aborted robbery of a Southern Pacific express train in which three crew members died, becomes known as the Siskiyou massacre and turns into one of the largest—and longest—manhunts in the region.

The famous "King of the Osage Hills" case brings the conviction of W. K. "Bill" Hale for the murder of Osage Indians for their oil properties. Agents posing as medicine men, cattlemen, and salesmen solve the murders. Their investigation is an early, highly-watched Bureau success.

○ May 25, 1928—Thomas Holden and Francis Keating, who pulled the successful 1926 mail truck hijacking at Evergreen Park, Illinois, and made away with $135,000 are convicted after eluding agents for two years and acquiring a reputation as one of the

The G-man and the Diamond King

most notorious holdup teams of the decade. They are arrested on a Kansas City golf course, armed only with their clubs.

November 1928—Training class (theory and practice) for newly appointed Special Agents and accountants is organized and located in Washington.

The case of Jerry Tarbot is successfully investigated in which Tarbot, claiming to be a world war veteran shell-shocked out of his memory, is found instead to be a draft dodger who spent the war years stealing automobiles in San Francisco.

March 27, 1929—Bureau agents arrest Al Capone in Florida when he fails to respond to a subpoena to appear as a witness in a federal Prohibition case in Chicago. He is later convicted of tax evasion.

May 10, 1929—All SACs required to visit all United States Attorneys in their respective jurisdictions at least once a month.

Most interesting cases for the year includes the breaking up of a nation-wide bankruptcy ring consisting of between fifteen and twenty Syrian merchants; and the case of the Chicago Association of Candy Jobbers, in which sixteen former officers and members are convicted of violating the Sherman anti-trust laws. The former business manager testifies that part of his duties had been to hire men to break out windows in tobacco stores that didn't belong to their association. The smashers were paid $15 per window.

June 1930—Manual of Investigations reprinted and revised.

The case of F. H. Smith Company of Washington, D.C., is investigated during this year involving millions of dollars, and resulting in the conviction of officials of the organization and disbarment proceedings against a prominent Washington, D. C. Attorney.

Important antitrust investigation results in forty-three members of the film Boards of Trade being restrained by injunction from forcing uniform lease contracts entered into by them.

December 31, 1930—Number of field offices increases to twenty-five.

April 9, 1931—New Bureau office established in Honolulu, territory of Hawaii.

◊ December 5, 1931—Bureau employees establish the Recreation Association, later
   renamed FBI Recreation Association, formed to promote athletic, social, and welfare
   for employees.

◊ March 1, 1932—Charles Lindbergh Jr. is kidnapped from his home in New Jersey.
   President Herbert Hoover authorizes the Prohibition Unit of the Treasury
   Department, the D.C. Police, and the Bureau to investigate, with Director Hoover
   coordinating the federal effort.
      International exchange of fingerprint data initiated with every important nation.

◊ May 1932—The first issue of the FBI's in-house magazine, *The Investigator*, consisting of
   two pages, is released.

◊ June 22, 1932—Federal kidnapping statute passes.

◊ July 1, 1932—Total number of field offices is reduced to twenty-two.
      All employees of the Bureau offered a correspondence course in accounting.
      Title of Bureau is changed to "United States Bureau of Investigation."

◊ July 8, 1932—Federal extortion statute passed.

◊ September 1, 1932—First issue of monthly bulletin entitled "Fugitives Wanted by
   Police." Renamed *FBI Law Enforcement Bulletin* in 1935.
      Bureau establishes a technical laboratory to assist investigations.

◊ September 19, 1932—First practical fingerprint course given to field employees.

◊ January 30, 1933—Course of training for Special Agents is increased from four to
   six weeks.

◊ February 15, 1933—Installation of Single Fingerprint file in the identification Unit
   is completed.

◊ June 10, 1933—By Executive Order, effective August 10, 1933, the Division of
   Investigation, U.S. Department of Justice, is created, absorbing the old United States

The G-man and the Diamond King

Bureau of Investigation, Prohibition Bureau, and Bureau of Identification. John Edgar Hoover named Director of the new Division and the Alcoholic Beverage unit formed as a separate unit with Assistant Director John S. Hurley as head.

July 23, 1933—George "Machine Gun" Kelly is captured by Bureau agents.

October 1, 1933—Collection of firearms and other interesting exhibits used by criminals from cases investigated by the Bureau is established.

December 26, 1933—Wilbur Underhill, "the Tri-State Terror" and one of the most sought-after criminals in Depression-era Oklahoma, engages in a holiday shootout in a rented cottage in Shawnee with two-dozen lawmen led by federal agents. Underhill escapes in his underwear, and although he is shot five times, manages to run sixteen blocks, break into a furniture store, and collapse on one of its beds. He's arrested and remains handcuffed to his hospital bed until he dies in early January. His last words: "Tell the boys I'm coming home."

January 17, 1934—The heir to the Schmidt Brewery fortune, Edward Bremer Jr., is captured by the notorious Barker-Karpis Gang. His family pays the $200,000 ransom, part of which was used to bribe police. Bremer, an excellent witness, helps federal agents by having memorized every detail of his kidnapping, even down to the wallpaper in the house where he was held. The Bureau's capture and prosecution of the gang is another feather in the Bureau's enhanced reputation and aids greatly in campaigns to thwart police corruption.

In 1934, the Division of Investigation solves every kidnapping case referred to it during the year.

February 20, 1934—Total number of field offices, twenty-four.

The total number of foreign countries with which fingerprints are exchanged totals fifty-five.

March 3, 1934—John Dillinger escapes from the Crown Point, Indiana, jail using what he later said was a wooden gun he'd carved himself—and the sheriff's car. It belonged to Lillian Holley, who was serving out her husband's term. Said Holley, reputed to be an excellent markswoman, "If I ever see John Dillinger again, I'll shoot him dead with my own pistol." The Bureau of the time thought women were best used as clerical workers, something that didn't change until Hoover was gone. Sheriff Holley would be pleased to note that nearly 2,000 of today's FBI Special Agents are women.

May/June 1934—A series of federal crime bills is passed by Congress. Their enforcement involves considerable additional work upon the Bureau. Legislation includes the federal reward bill; National Stolen Property act; crimes in connection with federal penal and correctional institutions; robbery of national banks and members banks of the Federal Reserve System; extortion; the federal anti-racketeering statute; power of arrest for Special Agents of the division, the right of the Special Agents to carry firearms; fleeing from one state to another to avoid prosecution or giving testimony in certain cases; killing or assaulting federal officers; amendment to the Federal Kidnapping Act of June 22, 1932.

July 1, 1934—Training for new Special Agents is increased from six to eight weeks. This training consists of studies in regulations, procedure, law, accounting, methodology, ethics, organization administration, fingerprint science, and scientific crime detection in the use of firearms.

Convictions number 3,531. The sentences impose eleven life sentences; 11,386 years, six months and seven days in actual, suspended in probationary sentences; fines total $772,938.73. The total value of recoveries affected in causes wherein employees of the Division perform investigative work amounts to $1,116,619.28.

Convictions are secured in 93.81 percent of all cases investigated brought to trial.

In addition to the 4,356 fugitives from justice located by the efforts of the Identification Unit during the year, Special Agents in the field locate 928 Federal fugitives.

The Identification Unit at this time begins its 36-hour service on all prints received.

July 22, 1934—Bureau agents kill John Dillinger outside the Biograph Theatre.

October 22, 1934—Charles Arthur "Pretty Boy" Floyd is killed by Bureau agents and police.

October 25, 1934—The new United States Department of Justice building is dedicated.

November 19, 1934—Training for new Special Agents increases to twelve weeks.

The G-man and the Diamond King

January 21, 1935—Retraining of experienced Special Agents over a four week period begins. This training is designed to keep agents abreast of new scientific investigative methods and technique; to increase their expertness in the use of firearms; and to afford an opportunity of studying enforcement methods in connection with recent federal legislation.

May 24, 1935—The five millionth fingerprint card is received at the identification division.

June 14, 1935—The Communication Section of the FBI is established. It includes four typewriters from which messages may be received and transmitted to the thirty-seven field offices simultaneously, or to a single office. Such an arrangement makes possible contact with all thirty-seven field offices within twelve minutes.

July 1, 1935—The Division of Investigation is formally renamed Federal Bureau of Investigation by Congressional enactment.

During the fiscal year 1935, there were 3,717 convictions, the imposed sentences totaled eight life sentences; and 10,757 years, eight months and four days in actual, suspended and probationary sentencing. Fines imposed amount to $333,974.68, the total savings and recoveries affected is $38,481,682.17, and the entire cost of operating the Bureau is $4,625,518. Convictions are secured in 94 percent of all cases brought to trial. Investigations successfully concluded during the year are those pertaining to the John Dillinger Gang, Mais-Legenza Tri-State Gang, Kansas City Massacre, Charles F. Urschel kidnapping, George Weyerhaeuser kidnapping, Charles A. Lindbergh Jr. kidnapping, and the Edward G. Bremer kidnapping.

July 29, 1935—FBI officials establish the FBI National Police Academy, forerunner of the FBI National Academy. The academy offers a twelve-week course in scientific and practical law enforcement methods to selected local and state police officers.

July 30, 1935—A course in physical instruction is added to the training school curriculum. The Bureau field offices total thirty-seven.

Endnotes

Introduction

1. Coy, Richard D., "Remembering an FBI Martyr," *Grapevine*, October 2008.

Prologue—The birth of modern crime-fighting

Sources used for the introductory essay include: Ackerman, Kenneth, "Five myths about J. Edgar Hoover," *The Washington Post*, November 9, 2011; Bloch, Don, "Bonaparte Founded G-Men," *Washington Star*, August 18, 1935; Burrough, Bryan, *Public Enemies* (London, England: Penguin Books, 2004);Hack, Richard, *Puppetmaster: The Life of J. Edgar Hoover* (Beverly Hills: New Millennium Press, 2004); Jeffreys-Jones, Rhodri, *FBI: A History* (New Haven: Yale University Press, 2007); Kessler, Ronald, *The FBI: Inside the World's Most Powerful Law Enforcement Agency* (New York: Pocket Books); Power, Richard Gid, *Broken: The Troubled Past and Uncertain Future of the FBI*, *New York:* Simon & Schuster, 2004); Weiner, Eric, "The Long, Colorful History of the Mann Act," http://www.npr.org/templates/story/story.php?storyId=88104308; Weiner, Tim, *Enemies: A History of the FBI* New York: Random House, 2012); and, of course, www.fbi.gov/about-us/brief-history.

Chapter 1—Dillinger, Public Enemies, and the G-Man

1. Perry, Douglas, *Eliot Ness: The Rise And Fall Of An American Hero* (New York: Penguin Group LLC, 2014), 23.
2. Hark, Ina Rae, *American Cinema of the 1930's: Themes and Variations* (New Jersey: Rutgers University Press, 2007), 12.
3. http://www.filmsite.org/littc.html; Spellman, Martin, "W.R. Burnett, American Realist," http://www.shotsmag.co.uk/feature_view.aspx?FEATURE_ID=118.
4. Clarens, Carlos, *Crime Movies: An Illustrated History* (New York: W.W. Norton & Company, Inc., 1980), 124.
5. www.fbi.gov/about-us/brief-history.
6. Yenne, Bill, *Tommy Gun* (New York: St. Martin Press, 2009), 4, 93 http://www.alcatrazhistory.com/mgk.htm.
7. Clarens, 127.
8. Burrough, Bryan, *Public Enemies* (London, England: Penguin Books, 2004), 16.
9. http://www.auto-ordnance.com/ao-thompson-submachine-gun.asp.
   http://www.wbez.org/episode-segments/thompson-submachine-gun-has-its-start-chicago.
   http://www.historyofwar.org/articles/weapons_thompson_submachinegun.html.
10. Vanderpool, Bill, "Bring Enough Gun: A History Of FBI Long Guns," *American Rifleman*, October 2013, 82.
11. Burrough, 136–137.
12. Ibid., 137.
13. www.fbi.gov/about-us/history/famous-cases/john-dillinger.
14. Burrough, 188, 237.
15. www.fbi.gov/about-us/history/famous-cases/john-dillinger.
16. http://Trintyvideo.net/tvcwallofhonor/Preloader.swf.
17. Burrough, 367–368.
18. Clarens, 122.
19. Burrough, 405–408.

20. Ibid., 408.

21. Purvis, Alston, *The Vendetta* (New York, NY: Public Affairs, 2005), 255–257.

22. Burrough, 477–478.

23. Smith, Hal H., "Agents of Justice Who Got Dillinger, *New York Times*, July 29, 1934, 130.

24. www.fbi.gov/about-us/brief-history/seal-motto.

Chapter 2—Nelson Klein, the original agent

1. www.dmna.ny.gov/nyg/

2. "Raymond Schindler Dies; Famed Private Detective," Associated Press, July 2, 1959.

3. *Hedgpeth, Tracy, "Raymond Schindler,"* http://www.imdb.com/name/nm2626621/bio?ref_=nm_ov_bio_sm.

4. Report by SAC J.H. Daly dated October 4, 1926, Interview of Nelson Klein, Klein FBI Personnel File 67-6822-Serial 15, 1, 2.

5. http://www.fbi.gov/portland/about-us/history-1/history.

6. Letter from SAC George J. Starr to Director Hoover, dated January 17, 1927, Klein FBI Personnel File 67-HQ-6822 serial 90, 1.

7. Efficiency rating Sheet from SAC George J. Star, March 31, 1927, Klein FBI Personnel File 67–HQ-6822 no serial number, 1.

8. Letter from SAC J.M. Tower to Director Hoover, dated June 17, 1927, Klein FBI Personnel File 67-HQ-6822 serial 44, 1.

9. Efficiency rating Sheet from SAC J. M. Tower, September 30, 1927, Klein FBI Personnel File 67–HQ-6822 no serial number, 1.

10. Letter from Director Hoover to Agent Klein, February 7, 1927, Klein FBI Personnel File 67-HQ-6822 serial 90, 1.

11. Letter from Director Hoover to Mr. J. L. Craven (SAC), dated May 28, 1927, Klein FBI Personnel File 67-HQ-6822 no serial number, 1.

12. Sicherman, Barbara, and Carol Hurd Green, editors, *Notable American Women: The Modern Period* (Cambridge: Harvard University Press, 1980)

13. *http://en.wikipedia.org/wiki/Mabel_Walker_Willebrandt;*
Rasmussen, Cecilia, "The Pioneering Career of Prohibition Portia," The Los Angeles Times, July 2, 2000.

14. "One more in the chain of Washington's baffling murder mysteries," *Gloversville (NY) Morning Herald*, 1936, found on *fultonhistory.com* site, New York State Digital Library.

15. "Chester Women Found Strangled," *Greenville News*, September 15, 1929, 1A.

16. "McPherson Goes Free: Jurors Fail To Indict," *Washington Post*, November 22, 1929, 1.

17. "Woman, 21, Took Her Own Life in Nation's Capital," *Concord Daily Tribune*, September 18, 1929, 1.

18. "McPherson Goes Free: Jurors Fail To Indict," *Washington Post*, November 22, 1929, 1.

19. *The Free Lance-Star*, Fredericksburg, Virginia, October 2, 1929.

20. "Formal Autopsy Report on Nurse Is Received Here," *Washington Post*, October 23, 1929, 24.

21. "McPherson Goes Free: Jurors Fail To Indict," *Washington Post*, November 22, 1929, 1, 5.

22. Letter from Director Hoover to Agent Klein, March 25, 1932, Klein FBI Personnel File 67-HQ-6822 serial 131, 1.

23. Efficiency Rating Sheet, from SAC W. M. Larson, dated March 31, 1932, Klein FBI Personnel File 67-HQ-6822 no serial number, 1.

24. Letter from Acting SAC W. A. Rorer, dated May 19, 1932, Klein FBI Personnel File 67-HQ-6822 serial 138, 1.

25. Memorandum from Inspector Vincent B. Hughes to Director Hoover, dated May 7, 1932, Klein FBI Personnel File 67-HQ-6822 no serial number, 1.

26. Memorandum from Inspector H.H. Clegg to Director Hoover, October 10, 1933, Klein FBI Personnel File 67-HQ-6822 serial 149, 1–3.

27. Ibid.

28. Efficency Rating Sheet, from SAC E. J. Connelley, dated March 31, 1934, Klein FBI Personnel File 67-HQ-6822 no serial number, 1, 2.

29. Letter from SAC E. J. Connelley to Director Hoover, dated May 23, 1934, Klein FBI Personnel File 67-HQ-6822 no serial number, 1.

30. "G-man in Labatt Case Shot To Death," *London Evening Advertiser*, August 19, 1935, 1.

31. Goldenberg, Susan, *Snatched! The Peculiar Kidnapping of Beer Tycoon John Labatt*, (Toronto: Dundurn Press, 2004), 1, 38.

32. "G-Man Slain By Car Thief Aided Canadian Officers Trail Kidnap Suspects," *London Free Press*, August 19, 1935, 1.

33. Goldenberg, 107.

34. Ibid., 126.

35. "Stoll Abduction Stirred Nation," *The New York Times*, October 17, 1934, 2.

36. "Federal Memorandum Reviews Hunt For Mrs. Stoll," *The New York Times*, October 17, 1934, 2 .

37. "Stoll Kin Demands the Death Penalty," *The New York Times*, October 22, 1934, 2.

38. "People & Events: Melvin Purvis, 1903-1960," http://www.pbs.org/wgbh/amex/dillinger/people events/p_purvis.html;

39. "Melvin Purvis Took Down Dillinger," http://www.crimemuseum.org/blog/melvin-purvis-the-man-who-took-down-dillinger

40. Bennett, Charles, "Legendary Lawman Melvin Purvis," http://www.officer.com/article/10283826/legendary-lawman-melvin-purvis

41. "Robinson Admits Stoll Kidnap Guilt after Coast Seizure," Associated Press, May 12, 1936.

42. Memorandum from Director Hoover to Mr. Tolson, dated March 22, 1935, Klein FBI Personnel File 67-HQ-6822 serial 166, 1.

43. Memorandum from Inspector H.H. Clegg to Director Hoover, April 5, 1935, Klein FBI Personnel File 67-HQ-6822 serial 168, 1.

44. Efficiency Rating Sheet, from SAC E.J. Connelley, dated May 6, 1935, Klein FBI Personnel File 67-HQ-6822 no serial number, 1.

45. Training School Report April/May 1934, McGovern FBI Personnel File 67-HQ-33945 serial 37, 1, 2.

46. Letter from SAC E. J. Connelley to Director Hoover, July 13, 1934, McGovern FBI Personnel File 67-HQ-33945 serial 40, 1.

47. Memorandum from Clyde Tolson to Director Hoover, June 22, 1935, McGovern FBI Personnel File 67-HQ-33945 serial 50, 1

48. Letter from Director Hoover to Agent McGovern, June 24, 1935, McGovern FBI Personnel File 67-HQ-33945 serial 51, 1

Chapter 3—Nemesis: George Barrett, mountain playboy

1. McQueen, Kevin, *Offbeat Kentuckians: Legends to Lunatics* (Kuttawa, KY: McClanahan Publishing House, 2001), 173.

2. McHone, Willard Thomas, *The Barrett Family of Clay County, Kentucky & Collateral Families* (Richmond, KY: University Book & Supply, 1997), 21.

3. Rankin, Victor R. "I killed a G-man now I hang," *Startling Detective Magazine*, May 1936, 32;

Lynch, Doria, "U.S. v. George Barrett," address, Seventh Annual Court History and Continuing Legal Education Symposium, Indianapolis, Indiana, November 7, 2014.

The G-man and the Diamond King

4. Rankin, 32.

5. Ibid.

6. Ibid.

7. Lynch, Doria.

8. Rankin, 32, 33.

9. Ibid.

10. Ibid.

11. Hersh, Richard, "Scourge of the Kentucky Hills," *Master Detective*, May 1939, 46.

12. Rankin, 32.

13. Hoover, J. Edgar, "The Meanest Man I Ever Knew," *The American Magazine*, April 1937, 137.

14. Dewey, C.C., Federal Bureau of Investigation, Summary Report dated August 25, 1935, 2.

15. Rankin, 32.

16. Hersh, 46.

17. Hoover, 138.

18. Hersh, 46.

19. Rankin, 33.

20. McHone, 56.

21. Hersh, 48.

22. Rankin, 33.

23. Ibid, 33.

24. Ibid, 33.

25. Hersh, 46, 48.

26. Death Penalty to be Demanded in G-Man's Slaying," *Cincinnati Times-Star*, August 17, 1935, 1.

27. Hersh, 48.

28. Hoover, 138, 139.

29. "Aged Jackson County Women Killed by Son," *Lexington Herald*, September 3, 1930, 1.

30. "Son Kills Aged Mother," *The Berea Citizen*, September 4, 1930, 1, 4.

31. "Aged Jackson County Women Killed by Son," *Lexington Herald*, September 3, 1930, 1.

32. "Aged Jackson County Women Killed by Son," *Lexington Herald*, September 3, 1930, 1, 6.

33. "Son Kills Aged Mother," *The Berea Citizen*, September 4, 1930, 1, 4.

34. "Aged Jackson County Women Killed by Son," *Lexington Herald*, September 3, 1930, 6.

35. "State Offers Reward for Arrest of Barrett," *Jackson County Sun*, September 11, 1930, 2.

36. "Search for Slayer," *Lexington Herald*, September 4, 1930, 1.

37. Rankin, 33.

38. McQueen, 177.

39. Hersh, 48.

40. McHone, 59.

41. Hersh, 75.

42. Rankin, 62.

43. Hersh, 75.

44. Ibid.

45. Hoover, 139.

46. Pearce, John, Ed., *Days of Darkness: The Feuds of Eastern Kentucky* (Lexington, KY: The University Press of Kentucky, 1994), 124.

47. Otterbein, Keith F., "Five Feuds: An Analysis of Homicides in Eastern Kentucky in the Late Nineteenth Century," *American Anthropologist*, June 2000, 237.

48. Pearce, 205.

49. Rankin, 62, 63.

50. Pearce, 206.

51. Dewey, C.C., Federal Bureau of Investigation, Summary Report dated August 25, 1935, Interview of Sheriff Filmore McIntosh and Police Judge W. C. Combs, FBI File 26-38858 serial 57, 2, 3.

52. Ibid, 5, Interview, Mrs. Will Parrott.

Chapter 4—The Cincinnati office eyes Barrett

1. Letter from Director Hoover to Joseph Nathan Kane, New York, NY, October 30, 1944, Klein FBI Personnel File 67-HQ-6822 serial 224, 1.

2. McGovern, Donald, Federal Bureau of Investigation, Summary Report dated August 18, 1935, Interview of Milton Tritsch, August 1, 1935, FBI File 26-38858 serial 38, 3.

3. Ibid., Interview of Ora P. Brown, August 14, 1935, 3.

4. McGovern, Donald, Federal Bureau of Investigation, Summary Report dated August 18, 1935, Interview of Scott Finley, August 14, 1935, FBI File 26-38858 serial 38, 4–5.

5. Ibid., Interview of Arthur Hock, August 14, 1935, 5–7.

6. Ibid., Interview of Andrew Wagner, August 15, 1935, 8.

7. Ibid., Interview of Thomas Farmer, August 15, 1935, 8.

8. Good, Meaghan, "1936: George W. Barrett, the first to hang for killing an FBI man," http://www.executedtoday.com/2013/03/24/1936-george-w-barrett-the-first-to-hang-for-killing-an-fbi-man/.

9. FBI Memorandum, "Digested History of the FBI," October 15, 1938, FBI File 62-24172 serial 153, 7, 11, 18.

10. "The FBI and the American Gangster," http://www.fbi.gov/about-us/history/a-centennial-history/fbi_and_the_american_gangster_1924–1938.

11. Mullin, T.J., "Colts and the Motorized Bandits," http://historicalgmen.squarespace.com/storage/Colts%20Motorized%20Bandits%20Summer2013.pdf.

12. Ibid.

13. "The FBI and the Thompson Submachine Gun," http://www.sofmag.com/fbi-and-thompson-submachine-gun.

14. Cheney, Peter, "Cars That Define Each Decade," *The Globe and Mail*, March 30, 2010. http://www.theglobeandmail.com/globe-drive/culture/commuting/cars-that-define-each-decade/article4312998/.

15. "What a Dandy Car You Make," *Letters of Note*, http://www.lettersofnote.com/.

16. Joseph Geringer, "Charles Arthur Floyd: 'Pretty Boy' from Cookson Hills," http://www.crimelibrary.com/gangsters_outlaws/outlaws/floyd/7.html.

17. "Charles 'Pretty Boy' Floyd," http://www.biography.com/people/charles-pretty-boy-floyd-9542085.

18. Fisher, Jeffery S., *The Life and Death of Pretty Boy Floyd* (Kent, OH: Kent State University Press, 1998).

19. "Kansas City Massacre—Charles Arthur "Pretty Boy" Floyd," http://www.fbi.gov/about-us/history/famous-cases/kansas-city-massacre-pretty-boy-floyd.

20. Ingram, Dale, "Family plot: Pretty Boy Floyd relative recalls his infamous uncle," *Tulsa World*, October 27, 2010.

21. www.fbi.gov/about-us/brief-history.

22. Ibid.

23. "The FBI and the Thompson Submachine Gun," http://www.sofmag.com/fbi-and-thompson-submachine-gun.

24. Ramsour II, Robert, "The FBI and the Thompson Submachine Gun," *Grapevine*, January 2010, 1.

25. Williams, Kevin, "The Pre-WWII Colt Super .38 Automatic," http://historicalgmen.squarespace.com/storage/colt%20super%20automatic.pdf.

The G-man and the Diamond King

Chapter 5— The shootout: August 16, 1935

1. McGovern, Donald C., Federal Bureau of Investigation Summary Report, August 18, 1935, FBI File 26-38858 serial 38, 8.
2. Nolan, Val, US Circuit Court of Appeals, For The Seventh Circuit, George W. Barrett v. US of America, Appellee's Brief 1936, 8.
3. McGovern, 11.
4. McKee, Samuel K., Federal Bureau of Investigation Summary Report, August 28, 1935, FBI File 26-38858 serial 73, 10.
5. Wheeler, Lonnie, "College Corner Journal; Singular Loyalty for Divided School," *The New York Times*, August 23, 1988.
6. McGovern, 11.
7. Nolan, 10.
8. McKee, 10.
9. McGovern, 11.
10. Nolan 10.
11. McKee, 10.
12. McGovern, 12.
13. Nolan, 10.
14. McKee, 10.
15. McGovern, 12.
16. Nolan, 11.
17. McKee, 10.
18. McGovern, 12.
19. Nolan, 11.
20. McKee, 10.
21. McGovern, 12.
22. Nolan, 11.
23. McKee, 10.
24. Nolan, 12.
25. McGovern, 14.
26. Hoover, J. Edgar, "The Meanest man I Ever Knew", *The American Magazine*, April 1937, 41.
27. McKee, Samuel K., Federal Bureau of Investigation Summary Report dated August 27, 1935, Investigation by Agent Charles B. Winstead, FBI File 26-38858 serial 59,6, 7.
28. Remsen, Douglas B., Report of Autopsy, dated August 16, 1935, 1, 2.
29. Nolan, 12, 13.
30. Ibid 13.
31. McKee, 12 (Interview of George W. Barrett, August 21, 1935)
32. McKee, Samuel K., Federal Bureau of Investigation Summary Report dated August 27, 1935, Investigation by Agent Charles B. Winstead, FBI File 26-38858 serial 59, 6, 7.
33. "Naming the FBI," http://historicalgmen.squarespace.com/naming-the-fbi/
34. "How the FBI Got its Name," http://www.fbi.gov/news/stories/2006/march/fbiname_022406.

Chapter 6— Aftermath: the bureau goes to work

1. Memorandum from Director J. Edgar Hoover to Mr. Nathan and Mr. Tolson, dated August 16, 1935, Klein FBI Personnel File 67-HQ-6822 serial 172, 1.
2. "G-man in Labatt Case Shot To Death," *The London Evening Advertiser*, August 19, 1935, 1.

3. "Last Rites Held for U.S. Agent," Federal Officials Send Many Floral Tributes, *Cincinnati Times-Star*, August 21, 1935, 23.

4. Letter from Indianapolis SAC H.H. Reinecke to Director Hoover dated August 21, 1935, FBI File 26-38858 serial 31, 1.

5. Letter from Indianapolis SAC H.H. Reinecke to Director Hoover dated August 23, 1935, FBI File 26-38858 serial 68, 1.

6. Johnson, J.S. Federal Bureau of Investigation Summary Report, dated October 15, 1935, signed statement of Irvin Brockman dated October 9, 1935, FBI File 26-38858 serial 127, 2–4.

7. McKee, Samuel K., Federal Bureau of Investigation Summary Report, dated August 24, 1935, signed statement of Mabel Barrett dated August 17, 1935, FBI File 26-38858 serial 52, 36, 37.

8. McKee, Samuel K., Federal Bureau of Investigation Summary Report, dated August 26, 1935, signed statement of George Barrett dated August 18, 1935, FBI File 26-38858 serial 70, 3–5.

9. McKee, Samuel K., Federal Bureau of Investigation Summary Report, dated August 27, 1935, signed statement of Edna Barrett dated August 26, 1935, FBI File 26-38858 serial 59, 12.

10. Ibid., 12, 13.

11. Ibid., 13.

12. Harrington, E.B. Federal Bureau of Investigation, Laboratory Report dated September 17, 1935, FBI file 26-HQ-38858 serial 116, 1.

13. Johnson, J.S., Federal Bureau of Investigation Summary Report dated October 15, 1935, signed statement of Irvin Brockman dated October 9, 1935, FBI file 26-HQ-38858 serial 125, 2, 3.

14. Ibid.

Chapter 7– The U.S. vs. George Barrett

1. Not Gulity Plea in G-Man Slaying" Indianpolis News, November 05, 1935, 1.

2. Lynch, Doria, "U.S. v. Barrett Presentation," Seventh Annual Court History and Continuing Legal Education Symposium, Indianapolis, November 7, 2014.

3. "Not Gulity Plea in G-Man Slaying," *Indianpolis News*, November 05, 1935, 1.

4. "G-Man Killer Suspect May Die in Noose, " *Indianapolis Times*, November 5, 1935, 1.

5. Memorandum from SAC Harold H. Reinecke to Director Hoover, dated October 12, 1935, 1, FBI File 26-38858 serial 123.

6. Memorandum from Special Agent J.E. Jones to SAC Harold H. Reinecke, dated October 19, 1935, 1, FBI File 26-38858 (no serial number legible).

7. Hoover, J. Edgar, "The Meanest man I Ever Knew," *The American Magazine*, April 1937, 140,141.

8. "Doctors Also Testify At Trial of Barrett," *Indianapolis News*, December 2, 1935, 3.

9. "Slaying Of G-Man Related To Jury," *Indianapolis Star*, December 3, 1935, 1.

10. Ibid, 2.

11. Ibid, 2.

12. "Klein's Bloodstained Clothing Shown Jury," *Indianapolis News*, December 3, 1935, 1,5.

13. "U.S. Evidence Piled Higher in Barrett Case," *Indianapolis Star*, December 4, 1935, 3.

14. Stuart N. Lake, *Wyatt Earp: Frontier Marshal* (New York: Houghton Mifflin, 1931).

15. Jeremy Agnew, *The Old West in Fact and Film: History Versus Hollywood* (Jefferson, North Carolina, McFarland & Company, Inc., 2012), 172.

16. "Klein's Bloodstained Clothing Shown Jury," *Indianapolis News*, December 3, 1935, 1, 5.

17. McKee, Samuel, K., Federal Bureau of Investigation Summary Report, August 28, 1935, 14,15.

18. "Klein's Bloodstained Clothing Shown Jury," *Indianapolis News*, December 3, 1935, 5.

19. "Barrett's Cousin is Unwilling Witness for U.S. in Trial of G-Man's Slayer, Nolan Claims," *Indianapolis Times*, December 4, 1935, 1, 3, 4.

The G-man and the Diamond King

20. Ibid., 1, 3.

21. U.S. Court of Appeals For the Seventh Circuit, George W. Barrett vs U.S. of America, Appeal From the District Court, Indianapolis, Indiana, Case No. 5718, March 17, 1936, 8,9.

22. "Barrett Confession Put In Record," *Indianapolis Star*, December 5, 1935, 1.

23. McKee, Samuel, K., Federal Bureau of Investigation Summary Report, August 28, 1935, FBI File 26-38858 serial 73, 13.

24. "Just Plain Curiosity," *Cincinnati Enquirer*, August 18, 1935, 18.

25. McKee 14.

26. "U.S. Evidence Piled Higher In Barrett Case," *Indianapolis Star*, December 4, 1935, 1–3.

27. "Stool Pigeon Takes Stand in Barrett Trial," *Indianapolis Star*, December 4, 1935, 1.

28. "Statement Tells Of Klein Slaying," *Indianapolis Star*, December 5, 1935, 1.

29. "Barrett Family Pride in Gun Skill Shown," *Indianapolis News*, December 5, 1935, 1.

30. "Feared G-Man Barrett Admits On Stand," *Indianapolis Star*, December 7, 1935, 14.

31. Ibid.

32. "G-man's Killer Makes Plea of Self-Defense," *Indianapolis Times*, December 6, 1935, 2.

33. "Feared G-Man Barrett Admits On Stand," *Indianapolis Star*, December 7, 1935, 14.

34. "Barrett Confession Put In Record," *Indianapolis Star*, December 5, 1935, 12.

35. Ibid.

36. Lynch, Doria, "U.S. v. Barrett Presentation," Seventh Annual Court History and Continuing Legal Education Symposium, Indianapolis, November 7, 2014.

37. "First slayer doomed by new Federal law," *The New York Times*, December 8, 1935, 46.

38. "Final Pleas Made In Barrett Trial," *The Indianapolis News*, December 7, 1935, 1.

39. Lynch, Doria.

40. "Noose Verdict Is First Under New U.S. Law," *Indianapolis Star*, December 8, 1935, 1.

41. Newton, Michael, *The Encyclopedia of Robberies, Heists, and Capers* (New York: Facts On File Inc., 2002), 55–56.

42. "John Paul Chase: bootlegger, thief, artist," http://www.babyfacenelsonjournal.com/john-paul-chase.html.

43. "Noose Verdict Is First Under New U.S. Law," *Indianapolis Star*, December 8, 1935, 1.

44. Ibid.

45. Message from Director Hoover to USA Val Nolan dated December 7, 1936, 1, FBI File 26-38858 serial 180, 1.

46. "Nolan Work Lauded By Chief of G-Men," *Indianapolis Star*, December 8, 1935, 1.

Chapter 8— George Barrett's last mile

1. "The execution of George Barrett," www.indystar.com/story/news/history/retroindy/2014/03/24/george-barrett/6830731/.

2. "Special Agent Nelson Bernard Klein," http://www.gcphs.com/LODD/Klein.html.

3. "Barrett Death by Hanging for March 24," *Indianapolis Star*, December 15, 1935, 1.

4. Lynch, Doria, "U.S. v. Barrett Presentation," Seventh Annual Court History and Continuing Legal Education Symposium, Indianapolis, November 7, 2014.

5. "First execution by electric chair," http://www.history.com/this-day-in-history/first-execution-by-electric-chair.

6. Miller, Wilbur R , editor, *The Social History of Crime and Punishment in America: An Encyclopedia* (Thousand Oaks, California: Sage Publications, 2012), 736–738.

7. "Forms of execution in the U.S.," http://deathpenalty.procon.org/view.resource.php?resourceID=001623.

8. "Turnpike killers among small group sentenced to federal death penalty," *Palm Beach Post*, March 31, 2009.

9. Lynch, Doria.

10. "Kentucky Slayer of G-Man Is Hanged," *Cincinnati Enquirer*, March 24, 1936, 1.

11. "Slayer of U.S. Agent Hanged after He Discusses Execution," *Chicago Daily Tribune*, March 24, 1936, 9.

12. Veselenak, Aaron, "The execution of Anthony Chebatoris," http://murderpedia.org/male.C/images/chebatoris_anthony/chebatoris.pdf.

13. "Anniversary of the last public hanging in America," http://paths2peace.blogspot.com/.

14. Gillespie, Kay L., *Executed Women of 20th and 21st Centuries* (Lanham, Maryland: University Press of America, 2009), 14–15.

15. McHone, Willard Thomas, *The Barrett Family of Clay County, Kentucky & Collateral Families*. (Richmond, KY: University Book & Supply, 1997), 67.

16. "Slayer of G-Man Becomes Catholic," *Indianapolis Times*, February 5, 1936, 1.

17. "Barrett Is Hanged for Slaying of G-Man; Shares Meal with Cat; Carried Last Mile," *Cincinnati Post*, March 24, 1936.

18. "Kentucky Slayer of G-Man is Hanged," *Cincinnati Enquirer*, March 24, 1936, 1.

19. "The Hanging of George Barrett…How Marion County's Last Execution Became a Nightmarish Rome Holiday," *Indianapolis Star*, February 13, 1977, 2 Sec. 5.

20. Ibid, 2.

21. Ibid, 2.

22. Ibid, 2.

23. "Murderer of G-Man Is Hanged In Indiana," *New York Times*, March 24, 1936, 46.

24. "The Hanging of George Barrett…How Marion County's Last Execution Became a Nightmarish Rome Holiday," *Indianapolis Star*, February 13, 1977, 2 Sec. 5.

25. Ibid, 2.

26. "Deputy Jerks Trap, Job None Wanted," *Indianapolis Star*, March 24, 1936, 1.

27. "Services Held For Barrett," *Indianapolis Star*, March 25, 1936, 1.

28. "Barrett Hanging Cost to U.S. Is $245.26," *Indianapolis Star*, April 11, 1936.

Chapter 9— The Director takes care of his own

1. Letter from director Hoover to Mrs. Klein, dated January 9, 1936, Klein FBI Personnel File 67-HQ-6822 no serial number.

2. Letter from Director Hoover to Mrs. Klein, dated January 28, 1936, Klein FBI Personnel file 67-HQ-6822 serial 203.

3. Letter from SAC R. Whitley to Director Hoover, dated March 26, 1936, Klein FBI Personnel file 67-HQ-6822 serial 212.

4. Letter from Director Hoover to Mrs. Klein, dated May 11,1936, Klein FBI Personnel file 67-HQ-6822 serial 209.

5. "Who was Brent Spence?" http://www2.cincinnati.com/news/bridge/brent spence.html.

6. Horstman, Barry, "Congressman's influence spanned decades," published by the *Cincinnati Post*, 1999, 90–91.

7. Letter from Mrs. Klein to Director Hoover, dated May 16, 1936, Klein FBI Personnel file 67-HQ-6822 no serial number.

8. Letter from Mrs. Klein to Director Hoover, dated July 14, 1936, Klein FBI Personnel file 67-HQ-6822 serial 215.

9. Letter from SAC R. Whitley to Director Hoover, dated September 11, 1936, Klein FBI Personnel file 67-HQ-6822 serial 216.

The G-man and the Diamond King

10. Memorandum from Assistant Director Tolson to Director Hoover, dated December 23, 1936, Klein FBI Personnel file 67-HQ-6822 serial 217.

11. Memorandum from Inspector T.D. Quinn to Assistant Director Tolson, dated December 27, 1936, Klein FBI Personnel file 67-HQ-6822 serial 218.

12. Letter from Mrs. Klein to Director Hoover, dated November 27, 1938, Klein FBI Personnel file 67-HQ-6822 serial 219 .

13. Letter from Director Hoover to Mrs. Klein, dated December 8, 1938, Klein FBI Personnel file 67-HQ-6822 no serial number.

14. Letter from SAC Herold H. Reinecke to Director Hoover, dated April 27, 1939, Klein FBI Personnel file 67-HQ-6822 serial 220.

15. Letter from Mrs. Klein to Director Hoover, dated June 25, 1944, Klein FBI Personnel file 67-HQ-6822 serial 221.

16. Letter from Director Hoover to Mrs. Wright, dated July 7, 1944, Klein FBI Personnel file 67-HQ-6822 no serial number.

Chapter 10—Epilogue

1. Letter from U.S. Attorney Val Nolan to Director Hoover, dated December 12, 1935, McGovern FBI Personnel File 67-HQ-33945 no serial number.

2. Letter from SAC H.H. Reinecke to Director Hoover, dated December 10, 1935, FBI File 26-38858 serial 202X.

3. Donald C. McGovern obituary, *Santa Monica Outlook*, April 14, 1966, 3.

4. Interview of Richard C. Klein on May 15, 2014, by Retired Special Agent Kevin G. Hogan at Saint Cloud, Florida.

5. Catharine Wright obituary, *Wooster Daily Record*, April 23, 1987, 13.

6. Source: Former Special Agent William R. Hargreaves at Cincinnati, Ohio.

7. Lt. Nelson "Bud" Klein Jr. obituary, *Bulloch Herald*, June 5, 1969.

8. Barbara Ann Klein Fleischman obituary, *Mount Vernon (O.) News*, July 31, 1978.

Chronology

FBI, USDOJ, Memorandum , "Digested History of the FBI," October 15, 1938, 8–15, FBI File Number 62-24172 serial number 153.

"1938—Intricacies of FBI History," courtesy Larry Wack and www.historicalgmen.squarespace.com.

Theoharis, Athan G., *The FBI: A Comprehensive Reference Guide*, The Oryx Press, 2000.

Photograph and illustration credits

107 Archdiocese of Indianapolis
108 Indiana State Library, Indianapolis
109 *Indianapolis Star*
114 courtesy Richard Klein
116 Archives and Rare Books Library, University of Cincinnati
120 courtesy Richard Klein
122 National Law Enforcement Officer Memorial, Washington, D.C.
123 courtesy Richard Klein
124 courtesy Michael McGovern
126 courtesy Richard Klein

Bibliography

Books

Alder, Dennis, *Colt Single Action: From Patersons to Peacemakers* (Edison, NJ: Chartwell Books, 2008).

Burrough, Bryan, *Public Enemies* (London, England: Penguin Books, 2004).

Clarens, Carlos, *Crime Movies: An Illustrated History* (New York: W.W. Norton & Company, Inc., 1980).

Flayderman, Norm, *Flayderman's Guide to Antique American Firearms and Their Values* (Iola, WI: Krause Publications, 2001).

Gentry, Curt J, *Edgar Hoover: The Man and The Secrets* (New York: W.W. Norton & Company, Inc., 1991).

Goldenberg, Susan, *Snatched: The Peculiar Kidnapping of Beer Tycoon John Labatt* (Toronto: DundurnPress, 2004).

Hack, Richard, *Puppetmaster: The Secret Life of J. Edgar Hoover* (Beverly Hills: New Millennium Press, 2004).

Hark, Ina Rae, editor, *American Cinema of the 1930s: Themes and Variations* (New Brunswick, NJ: Rutgers University Press, 2007).

McHone, Willard Thomas, *The Barrett Family of Clay County, Kentucky & Collateral Families* (Richmond, KY: University Book & Supply, 1997).

McQueen, Kevin, *Offbeat Kentuckians: Legends to Lunatics* (Kuttawa, KY: McClanahan Publishing House, 2001).

Nathan, Miller, *Theodore Roosevelt: A Life* (New York: William Morrow and Company Incorporated, 1992).

Newton, Michael, *The Encyclopedia of Robberies, Heists, and Capers* (New York: Facts On File Inc., 2002).

Pearce, John Ed, *Days of Darkness: The Feuds of Eastern Kentucky* (Lexington, KY: The University Press of Kentucky, 1994).

Perry, Douglas, *Eliot Ness: The Rise And Fall Of An American Hero* (New York: Penguin Group LLC. 2014).

Purvis, Alston, *The Vendetta* (New York, NY: Public Affairs, 2005).

Weiner, Tim, *Enemies: A History of the FBI* (New York: Random House Publishing Group, 2012).

Yenne, Bill, *Tommy Gun* (New York: St. Martin's Press, 2009).

Magazines

Clapp, Wiley, "Not Just A .45," *American Rifleman*, April 2013.

Coy, Richard D., "Remembering An FBI Martyr," *Grapevine*, October 2008.

"Crippled Killer," *Time*, December 30, 1935.

Curtis, Wayne, "Bootleg Paradise," *American Heritage*, April/May 2007.

Hersh, Richard, "Scourge of the Kentucky Hills," *Master Detective*, May 1939.

Hoover, J. Edgar, "The Meanest Man I Ever Knew," *The American Magazine*, April 1937.

Nineteenth Century," *American Anthropologist*, June 2000.

Otterbein, Keith F, "Five Feuds: An Analysis of Homicides in Eastern Kentucky in the Late Nineteen Century," *American Anthropologist*, June 2000.

Ramsour II, Robert, "The FBI and the Thompson Submachine Gun," *Grapevine*, January 2010.

Rankin, Victor R. "I killed a G-man now I hang," *Startling Detective Magazine*, May 1936.

Williams, Kevin, "The Pre-WWII Colt Super .38 Automatic," *Man At Arms*, June 2009.

Newspapers

The Berea Citizen; Chicago Daily Tribune; Cincinnati Enquirer; Cincinnati Times-Star; The Concord Daily Tribune; Indianapolis News; Indianapolis Star; Indianapolis Times; Jackson County Sun; Jacksonville Journal; Kentucky Post; Lexington Herald; London Evening Advertiser; London Free Press; Louisville Courier-Journal; and The New York Times.

The G-man and the Diamond King

About the author

William Eric Plunkett was born in Oswego, New York and graduated from Bishop Cunningham High School. He is a graduate of Mohawk Valley Community College, Utica, New York and the State University of New York at Oswego where he obtained a Bachelor of Arts in Public Justice in 1981.

In 1982 he entered the FBI at Albany, New York, and later was assigned to offices in Syracuse, New York; Cincinnati, Ohio; and Washington, D.C. In Washington, he was involved in joint Counterintelligence operations with the Central Intelligence Agency, and in Cincinnati he investigated National Security (Counterintelligence, Terrorism, and Cyber) matters. He was an original member of the Cincinnati FBI Joint Terrorism Working Group and later with the FBI Joint Terrorism Task Force, which was formed after 9/11. He served on the Executive Board of the Hamilton County Police Association in 2007 and 2008, leaving government service in 2011.

Bill is a lifetime member of the Fraternal Order of Police, a member of the Society of Former Special Agents of the FBI, The Knights of Columbus, and also the Federal Law Enforcement Officers Association.

He has been living in downtown Cincinnati, Ohio since 1997 and enjoys golf, kayaking, and cycling. He has been previously published in the FBI's in-house magazine, *The Investigator*. This is his first book.